Prayers God Always Answers

Prayers God Always Answers

HOW HIS FAITHFULNESS

SURPRISES, DELIGHTS, AND AMAZES

by Nancy Kennedy

WATERBROOK
PRESS

PRAYERS GOD ALWAYS ANSWERS
PUBLISHED BY WATERBROOK PRESS
5446 North Academy Boulevard, Suite 200
Colorado Springs, Colorado 80918
A division of Random House, Inc.

All scripture quotations, unless otherwise indicated, are taken from the *Holy Bible,
New International Version*®. NIV® Copyright © 1973, 1978, 1984 by International Bible
Society. Used by permission of Zondervan Publishing House. All rights reserved.
Scripture quotations marked (MSG) are taken from *The Message.* Copyright © by
Eugene H. Peterson 1993, 1994, 1995. Used by permission of NavPress Publishing Group.
Scripture quotations marked (AMP) are taken from *The Amplified Bible,* Old Testament.
Copyright © 1965, 1987 by The Zondervan Corporation. *The Amplified New Testament,*
copyright © 1954, 1958, 1987 by The Lockman Foundation. Used by permission.
Scripture quotations marked (TLB) are taken from *The Living Bible* copyright © 1971. Used by
permission of Tyndale House Publishers, Inc., Wheaton, Illinois 60189. All rights reserved.
Scriptures marked (KJV) are taken from the *King James Version* of the Bible. Scriptures marked
(NKJV) are taken from the *New King James Version.* Copyright © 1982 by Thomas Nelson, Inc.
Used by permission. All rights reserved. Scriptures marked (NASB) are taken from the
New American Standard Bible®. © Copyright The Lockman Foundation 1960, 1962,
1963, 1968, 1971, 1972, 1973, 1975, 1977. Used by permission.

Grateful acknowledgment is extended to Discovery House Publishers for permission to
reprint the passages included herein from *My Utmost for His Highest* by Oswald Chambers.
Copyright © 1935 by Dodd Mead & Co., renewed © 1963 by the Oswald Chambers
Publications Association Ltd. Discovery House Publishers, Box 3566, Grand Rapids, MI, 49501.
All rights reserved.

ISBN 1-57856-197-3

Library of Congress Cataloging-in-Publication Data
Kennedy, Nancy, 1954-
    Prayers God always answers / by Nancy Kennedy. — 1st ed.
      p. cm.
    ISBN 1-57856-197-3
    1. Prayer—Christianity.   I. Title.
BV210.2.K45 1999
248.3'2—dc21   99-26108
                                         CIP

Printed in the United States of America
1999—First Edition
10 9 8 7 6 5 4 3 2 1

This book is dedicated to my dad,

for whom I pray,

and to my Father in heaven,

to whom I pray.

Contents

Acknowledgments

Each time I write a book, I look forward to writing this page because it's where I get to thank some of my favorite people for their help. They get to see their names in print, and it's a whole lot cheaper than paying them.

To Dan Rich and everyone at WaterBrook Press: I am honored you're willing to take a chance with me. To Erin Healy, my editor: brown sugar cinnamon Pop Tarts all around! May all the calories be removed.

To David and Heather Kopp: Thank you for taking your time to brainstorm with me and be my friends. You are two of my favorite people in the universe.

To phil.callaway@somewhereinthefrozentundra.net: Thank you for being. Um, I mean, thank you for being an encouragement to me. I'll fax you a check.

To Jim Cole, a.k.a. "Hey, Theology Man!" and Ron "Bible Answer Guy" Brown, my personal pastors: Thank you so much for your theological help. I owe you both a year's worth of sermon illustrations. Thanks, too, to Ray Cortese, senior pastor at Seven Rivers Presbyterian Church in Lecanto, Florida. Much of what I write I "glean" from you. (Unless, of course, gleaning is illegal.)

To all the women who love and support me (you know who you are) and to JoAnna and Alan Woody, who pray for me: With all my heart I appreciate you.

I especially appreciate my faithful readers. I prayed for you before I wrote this book because I wrote it *just for you.*

Thanks to my family for letting me hole up in my office and play that *awful classical music* and forget to cook dinner and neglect you horribly one more time while I write one more book. Thank you too for being the odd characters that you are and for giving me things to write about. "The LORD bless you and keep you; the LORD make His face shine upon you and be gracious to you; the LORD turn His face toward you and give you peace" (Numbers 6:24-26).

Most of all I thank Almighty God, who mercifully calls me his child. Father, I am not worthy, but I am grateful. *For I know that my Redeemer lives!*

Introduction

I haven't told anybody this, but I have a secret prayer. Every night before I go to sleep, I pray that I will wake up with a body like Cindy Crawford's. I pray that the noise my car makes will magically go away and that the pile of Hershey's Kisses I ate earlier that evening won't go directly to my thighs. I pray that one day I'll open the front door and someone will push a refrigerator-size check in my face and say, "Nancy Kennedy, you've just won eleven million dollars! What are you going to do first?" The trouble is, even though I'm fully prepared to have a gorgeous figure and I've been practicing shouting, "I'm going to Disney World!" God's not answering those prayers.

This is not a new phenomenon either. I've prayed for years, and it seems all circuits to heaven are either busy or disconnected. Take the time I was a new Christian with a busy toddler under my feet. Daily I'd beg, "Lord, give me patience." But instead of a sudden *poof!* and a euphoric, supernatural state of patient calmness overpowering me like I expected, Alison came down with chickenpox. I remember thinking, *Maybe God's not hearing me right*, and (once Alison's itching stopped) I asked again. That time she pulled all the knobs off the stereo, ate one of them, dumped laundry soap in the dishwasher, and shoved a grape up her nose.

"No, God!" I cried. "You don't understand—I don't want chaos, *I want patience!!!*"

So Alison smeared Vaseline on the bathroom mirror, unwrapped seven bars of soap, and hid my car keys.

About that time I decided to change my request altogether and ask God for a deeper trust in him (again, expecting a *poof!* experience). Ahhh, no chickenpox or slimy mirrors. That time he sent morning sickness…but not before my husband lost his job. It didn't take long for me to realize my prayers weren't working. Not only that, they often left me looking into the skies, scratching my head and wondering, *Are you even up there, God?*

But then there are other times, times when I *know:* Not only is he up there, but he hears my SOS. Just a few weeks ago, I discovered a forty-dollar error in my checkbook—an error that left me in the red. After I whined and fretted for an hour or so over my predicament, as a last resort I prayed. Not long after that a neighbor rode up to my house on his bicycle and asked if he could buy four copies of one of my books. Then he handed me a check for forty dollars. Bingo! *Poof!* Instant answer to my prayer.

Since then I've been puzzled. Why do I get an immediate *poof!* answer one time and a toddler with chickenpox the next? Why do some prayers go unanswered? What about my motivation—will God answer me if I'm not convinced he's even listening? Does he need my prayers? Would he have sent the man on the bicycle to my house even if I hadn't prayed? After much thought, I've come to the conclusion that I don't know beans about prayer.

Like you, I've heard all the sayings and have seen all the wall posters and needlepointed platitudes: *Prayer changes things. A day hemmed in prayer will not easily unravel. Life is short; pray hard.* But why? God is God, and he does what he wants, right? He doesn't need my puny prayers.

Yet he tells me to pray.

It's not as if I can twist his arm or make him change his mind with my prayers…*yet he tells me to pray.* He says, "Ask and it will be given to you; seek and you will find; knock and the door will be opened to you" (Luke 11:9). Still, I don't pray as I should. I get discouraged when I don't get the answers I expect. So I pray more earnestly, with more faith and greater thanksgiving. I do everything the Bible says, and still God doesn't answer.

Or maybe he does.

Recently I sat down and made a list of prayers God *always* answers. It's a long list too. There's just one small catch: Prayers for quick riches, fame, and long, lanky legs didn't make the list (at least not my list). Instead, the prayers on my list that God always answers are the ones that bring glory to him (and not to me), prayers that refine my character and make me fit for his kingdom. And although his answers are rarely what I expect, they are always what I need. That explains why my kids get chickenpox when I pray for patience, why I'll probably never get to shout, "I'm going to Disney World!" on national TV, and why I'll keep waking up in my own body instead of Cindy Crawford's.

What about you? What are you praying for? Like me, do you sometimes ask for one thing and seem to get another? While I don't presume to know what God is doing, I do know this: He will not give a stone to one of his children who asks him for bread (Matthew 7:9). He's a loving Father, and you need never be afraid to come to him with your requests.

It bears repeating: God doesn't need my prayers, but I need my prayers. I need to pray so that when the answers come, I'm left in awe, saying, "There really is a God! He really does listen to his children!" Not only that, God invites—even commands—me to pray. I don't have to fully understand it; all I have to do is do it.

It's my prayer for you that within the pages of this book you'll be both entertained and encouraged. I've included some thought- and discussion-provoking questions and quotes from noted Christian leaders and thinkers at the end of each chapter. Maybe you and a prayer partner or friend could use them to help disciple one another and deepen your prayer life. Or you could use them for a group Bible study. (I hope you'll at least read them and not skip over them like I'm sometimes tempted to do with similar material.)

As for the whole subject of prayer, I'll tell you right up front: I don't know all the answers. (Most of the time I even get the questions wrong.) But I do know this: Prayer moves mountains. It calms storms. It feeds multitudes and helps a frantic mother find a set of car keys. It puts the pray-er in touch with the God who made her.

Prayer definitely changes things. Prayer changes *me*.

ONE

Confessions of a Prayer Wimp

What men usually ask for when they pray to God
is that two and two may not make four.

RUSSIAN PROVERB

To begin a book on prayer, this is probably where I'm supposed to tell you all about my incredible prayer adventures, or at least my disciplines. How I get up before dawn each morning in eager anticipation of meeting the Lord in our special place, and how I begin with a time of quiet meditation and worship. I'm probably supposed to add that I never doubt that God hears me because I always check my motivation and confess every sin before I pray. And then I think I'm supposed to tell you how I pray in absolute, unwavering faith and how I go through my day not only remembering what I've prayed but waiting expectantly for God's answers (for which I've already thanked him).

But I'd rather tell you the truth.

I don't remember the exact circumstances, but my prayer life began back in elementary school. I loved David Easter, but so did Nancy Vernon. Since she was prettier than I, I would pray that (1) I could be prettier, (2) the packs of gum I slipped into David's desk would act as irresistible love charms, or (3) Nancy would move away.

Unbelievably, Nancy's father was transferred to Virginia, and I never saw her again. Unfortunately David loved kickball more than either one of us, so my prayers were only half answered. Still, I figured I was onto something.

In seventh grade I prayed that Paul Minardi would ask me to go steady (he did), and then in eighth grade I prayed that either Scott Kelly or Bob Richardson would (they didn't). In ninth grade I did something incredibly stupid while on vacation with my parents. I snuck out of the house where we were staying to be with an older guy I was forbidden to see. I got caught—and then I prayed. This time my prayer was a passionate, fervent, breast-beating howling for mercy—but only because I had been caught and forced to spend the remainder of my vacation indoors while the rest of the family enjoyed the beach.

I think I stopped praying about that time, except for an occasional "Help me on my algebra test!" (I got Ds.) Prayer didn't mean a thing to me. It didn't help me in the least. The only thing it ever got me was extra points in my church religion class, where I could rattle off memorized prayers flawlessly in a single breath. *"OurFatherwhoartinheavenhallowedbethyname...."*

But as for having anything—even remotely—to do with real life, prayer wasn't on my list. All that changed, however, at 9:43 A.M. on May 30, 1978, in the ladies' room of the supply warehouse at Loring Air Force Base, Maine. With a woman named Rita, who held a New Testament in her hand, I prayed, "God, I don't even know what I'm doing, but all I know is, I'm sorry. I've made a mess of my life. I'm afraid of dying. I'm afraid of living. If you want me, you can have me."

Later I learned I'd prayed something called "the sinner's prayer." At the time all I knew was I'd finally come face to face with the God who answers prayers. *My* prayers. Except—I've come to discover he doesn't always answer them the way I would if I were God:

- I pray for strength. I get weakness, that his strength might be made perfect (2 Corinthians 12:9-10).
- I pray to be pretty. He leaves my face the way it is and makes me beautiful instead (2 Corinthians 3:18).
- I pray for perfection. He shows me my failures and teaches me how to be excellent (1 Corinthians 12:31).
- I pray for my husband to share my faith. He whispers, "Your Maker is your husband" (Isaiah 54:5), and gives me love enough to wait.
- I pray for enough money in my bank account so I'll never have to worry. He makes sure I have what I consider to be less than enough so I'll have to trust him (Philippians 4:19).
- I pray for a life filled with good things and laughter. He allows my car to break down and the cats to throw up on the rug and the dining-room chairs to break and the peskiest armadillo in the state to dig up our plants faster than we can plant them—all in order to show me my source of laughter comes not from a picture-perfect life but from his joy, which is my strength (Nehemiah 8:10).

I should tell you I don't normally have this philosophical, spiritual— even *mature*—attitude toward my prayers and God's answers. In fact, as I write this, I'm reeling from a weekend of answered prayer that I'd just as soon forget. I'll tell you more about it later. Let's just say, when you ask God to show you your sin that you may hate it as much as he does, it rarely involves a tap on the shoulder and a handwritten note on scented stationery. God showed me mine while I was on stage speaking at a women's dinner, and it involved pride, greed, self-centeredness, and lust for the bowl of chocolate-covered mints on one of the tables.

As painful as some of God's answers are, I know that every last one of them is given from a Father's heart of goodness and that he disciplines everyone whom he calls his child (Hebrew 12:10). That's why, after I'd finished speaking, I could retreat to my hotel room and sob to the God who knows me and loves me anyway and thank him for choosing a most inopportune and unlikely time to answer a prayer I'd prayed earlier in the week.

I wish I could tell you that I have God all figured out, especially when it comes to prayer, but of course I can't. I also wish I could tell you I have a strong, vibrant, dynamic prayer life, that I'm what's known as a "prayer warrior." To borrow a phrase from author Mary Pierce, I'm more of a "prayer wimp."[1] Most days I don't set aside quiet times to listen to the Lord and to learn of his heart. Or if I do, my mind instantly wanders until I find myself singing the latest McDonald's commercial or reciting over and over, "Remember to buy Tabasco sauce. Remember to buy Tabasco sauce...."

Then, thinking I've heard the voice of God, I move on to the *real* reason for my prayer time, The List: *Please let my car start today, and help me zip up my jeans that I accidentally put in the dryer on high. Please let the low-fat, premium ice cream be on sale today (and let there be Rocky*

Road), and help the phone bill not reflect until next month that forty-five-minute call I made to my sister. Bless my family, and make them all get along when I'm around because I really, REALLY don't want to deal with their petty bickering and turmoil. Let my day go smoothly, my hair not go flat, my thighs not jiggle, and my breath stay fresh…and bless all the missionaries around the world and all of our leaders and the starving children. Amen.

Once in a while I might tack on "in Jesus' name," especially if I'm afraid my jeans will be exceptionally snug. Sometimes I even ask for wisdom and guidance—but not consistently and not always in faith, believing God will answer. Although I always know he can, I'm not always sure he will.

Occasionally, though, I'm struck by God's awesomeness. I'm aware of his bigness, that he would stoop from heaven to bend his ear toward me. These are the moments in which prayer becomes communion rather than a presentation of a grocery list. It becomes a meeting of hearts rather than a clashing of wills. In these rare moments of worship, I'm swept away in total abandon. And it's in these times I find myself praying the prayers God always answers.

❧

Lord,

You welcome me into your presence as your much-loved child and offer your ear to my prayers. I confess that too often I think of you as merely a granter of wishes and not as the Person who first and foremost wants a relationship with me. Help me to remember that! "May the words of my

*mouth and the meditation of my heart be pleasing in your sight, O LORD,
my Rock and my Redeemer" (Psalm 19:14).*

THINK ON THESE THINGS

- What are some of your prayers, and how do you think God will answer them? If he doesn't answer as you expect, how will that affect your faith?

- Name some prayers you're afraid to pray. Why are you afraid? If you could ask God for anything, what would that be? Ask him.

- Meditate on Philippians 4:6-7, and use it as the basis for your own personal prayer.

- "Prayer enlarges the heart until it is capable of containing God's gift of himself. Ask and seek, and your heart will grow big enough to receive him and to keep him as your own."—Mother Teresa, quoted in *Pathway to the Heart of God*

---

[1] Mary Pierce, "Confessions of a Prayer Wimp," *Focus on the Family* magazine, date unknown.

PART ONE

Help Me

How gracious he will be when you cry for help!

As soon as he hears, he will answer you.

ISAIAH 30:19

Two

Blessed Are the Gullible —They Need It!

HELP ME BELIEVE

Those who stand for nothing will fall for anything.

ALEXANDER HAMILTON

For the most part, I've managed to stay clear of creating international incidents, which I think is an admirable trait in a person. Twenty years ago, however, I came close in what my husband refers to as the Canadian Milk Episode. But before I get to that, I need to tell you about my nearly thirty-year reigning title.

Although I don't mean to brag, in 1970 I was voted Miss Most Gullible at Christopher Columbus Junior High School in Canoga Park, California. As far as I know, no one has claimed my crown since.

From the time I could say, "Really?" I've believed just about every-thing anyone with a straight face has ever told me. I grew up believing my mom was a gypsy. My dad used to tell me that Mom had purple petticoats hanging in the back of her closet and then forbid me to go there. One time my brother almost convinced me that we should take a look, but the fear of the Gypsy's Revenge (which Dad never spelled out, merely hinting at its grisly consequences) kept me from further investigation.

Dad also said eating too many black olives would put hair on my chest. Since *he* had a hairy chest and *he* ate black olives, I put two and two together and ate carrot sticks instead. Even now as an adult, every time I eat black olives I'm tempted to sneak a peek down my shirt.

Now to the Canadian Milk Episode. I was in a restaurant with my husband, Barry, and two friends in New Brunswick, Canada, just across the Maine border from where we were stationed in the air force. After we had ordered dinner, Frank, our so-called friend, leaned over and whispered to me, "I forgot to warn you—Canadians don't pasteurize their milk." I figured he knew, being from near Canada himself.

So, not wanting to contract whatever it is you might contract by drinking unpasteurized milk, when the waitress came back with the glass I had ordered, I asked her if she had any American milk. "I heard you Canadians don't pasteurize your milk," I said, "and well, I have an American stomach."

As she looked at me as if I'd confessed to recently being abducted by aliens, my table companions burst out laughing. I still didn't see that Frank was putting one over on me. All I knew was I didn't want the contents of my American stomach being upset by foreign organisms, even if they were from an allied country.

I don't remember if I ever smoothed things over with the waitress (I ended up drinking the milk out of duty to my country), but I do know I never returned to Canada. For all I know, they've posted wanted posters up there with my picture on them and have labeled me America's Most Obnoxious Tourist. ("If you see this woman, whatever you do, *don't* offer her dairy products.")

You would think I should've known better since the Canadian Milk Episode came on the heels of the Flight Line Incident. As one of the newest troops in my air force unit, I once was sent by my supervisors to obtain a thousand yards of flight line from a remote supply depot near the runway. I had no idea what flight line was, only that I had to find some ASAP. I also had a requisition for sky hooks—one dozen. Little did I know sending a new troop out for flight line (another name for the runway) and sky hooks (hooks *for the sky?!*) was a favorite way of driving gullible people like me to distraction. Again, I should've known better. Just a year before, as a new shoe-store employee, I was sent in search of a wall stretcher to help our stockroom shelves accommodate the extra shoe boxes.

I'm the first to admit that I thoroughly enjoy being on the laughed-at end of snow snake and snipe hunts and even a search for a wall stretcher or two, but not all of my gullibility has resulted in amusing stories to pass on to my children. In high school I started looking for something—anything—to believe in, and I fell under the spell of a man who said he could guide me.

He wore a doctor's white coat and played the harpsichord and claimed to have The Answer. All he required was a letter explaining why I wanted his help and a check for seventy-five dollars. I gave him both, then went to his house, where he conducted Primal Therapy sessions. He told me to name an action that would represent the ultimate breakthrough for me—something I would never do unless I were totally Free. I'd heard that others had named taking off all their clothes. I didn't think I wanted that much Freedom, so I chose singing a fully clothed version of "Happy Birthday."

I sat in his overstuffed chair and poured my soul out for about an hour, then he looked at his watch and told me it was time to reach my screaming point. I held my breath as my heart pounded out of my chest. I knew (just as I had known my dad's stories were all true) that all I had to do was sing, and I would be Free. All the guilt and emptiness and yuck in my life would be gone with just one song.

So I sang as the man accompanied me on the harpsichord (included in the seventy-five dollars). Afterward he escorted me to the door, declared me Free, and mentioned that another session with him would cost another seventy-five dollars. I left feeling Freer than I had felt in years—until I got out to my car and realized I had been duped.

The following year I went to someone who tried to convince me all my problems in life were my dad's fault and then rolled me into a fetal position on his couch. Then someone else told me I needed to listen to my Inner Child and do what she says. *She* kept wanting to eat black olives, but since I'd developed a phobia over growing chest hair, I told my Inner Child to go home. That's when I vowed never to believe anything ever again.

Until someone told me the most far-fetched, outrageous story I had ever heard.

This time it turned out to be the truth.

Growing up in church, I'd heard the story before but not the way Rita told it to me. She told me as if she believed it, and when she read out of Romans and said, "Everyone who calls on the name of the Lord will be saved" (10:13), I believed it too.

Then I remembered that I was still the reigning Most Gullible from Christopher Columbus Junior High School and that I was a sucker for any new thought that came along. *Maybe this is just another theory*, I reasoned. But just in case it wasn't, I prayed, "Lord, I think I believe— please help my unbelief." The father of a demon-possessed boy who once came to Jesus for help had also prayed that same prayer, I later discovered.

Of all the prayers I've ever prayed, I think the request for proof of his existence is one that God is most eager to answer. *Jesus loves me, this I know, for the Bible tells me so.* On pages between pink, imitation leather covers, in black and white type, God spells out his story: a creation, a sin, many sins that follow. A plan to buy the sinners back. A sinless Son as a sacrifice. A death, a resurrection, an ascension into heaven, and a promise to come again for all who believe.

But how do I, the reigning Most Gullible, know it's true?

For one thing, I believe because the old me died the day I put my trust in Christ, and there's a new me in her place, a me I never dreamed could exist. The old me woke up angry and scared most of the time, dreading the day, marking the time until I died. That me cried a lot, but I never knew why. I wanted to be free, but I couldn't figure out what was keeping me bound. Despite having everything I could ever want, I was terribly unhappy—and terribly good at pretending I wasn't. Nothing worked. Nothing clicked. Nothing. *Nothing.*

The new me wakes up with a purpose, no longer angry, no longer dreading the day. *Genuinely* free. Free to love my husband, to enjoy my children. To pray, to read, to write, to worship. For the most part this new me is terribly happy. Things work, things click. And when they don't? I take comfort in knowing eventually, *ultimately*, all things will work together for good (Romans 8:28).

Sometimes I don't even remember the old me. At times my husband will bring up the contrast: "You were a mean little so-and-so back then," he'll say.

Yeah, I was.

I still am at times, but now I have Someone on my side, changing me from the inside out, helping me both to *want* to change and then actually to *do* it. You wouldn't want to have known the old me. This me is so much nicer to be around.

Even so, sometimes I have moments of doubt. *Come on! You expect me to buy the idea of heaven and hell, a flood that destroyed the earth, some poor guy getting swallowed by a fish, and a crucified Savior rising from the dead?* These moments are becoming fewer and farther between, but I still have them. And then something will happen: I'll see former-atheist-now-church-pastor Keeth Staton at Wal-Mart; I'll have every intention to bite my husband's head off, and instead I'll spout a blessing; I'll read the scripture where Jesus says, "Blessed are those who have not seen and yet have believed" (John 20:29), and I'll *know* he was talking about me. Evidence is all around me.

I used to think the trees made the wind blow. To me it was true *because I believed it.* But when I learned it was the other way around—that the wind blew the trees—I believed it because it was true.

Same thing with eating black olives. Same thing with believing in God.

❧

Lord,

Sometimes I don't know what to believe, especially when there are so many so-called truths vying for my attention. But you have given me your Word and your Holy Spirit, who leads me into all truth. Give me discernment, Lord, and help me believe your truth only. Amen.

THINK ON THESE THINGS

- What are some false beliefs that are presented as truth today? What makes them false? What are some of your beliefs about God? How did you come by them?

- In John 18:38, Pilate asks Jesus, "What is truth?" How would you answer him?

- The apostle Peter tells us to "always be prepared to give an answer to everyone who asks you to give the reason for the hope that you have" (1 Peter 3:15). How would you answer someone who asks you why you believe?

• "The mature believer is the one who has seen God act in direct and specific ways, whose faith cannot be shaken—ever—because it is built on fact."—Steve Brown, *Jumping Hurdles, Hitting Glitches, Overcoming Setbacks*

❦

THREE

The Day the Dot Turned Blue

HELP ME TRUST

Faith never knows where it is being led,
but it loves and knows the One Who is leading.

OSWALD CHAMBERS

Maybe I hadn't been specific enough. Maybe I should've asked for a do-over. After all, I only had a few minutes to answer the question: What do you want from God?

It was the start of a new Sunday-school year, and the teacher had asked us to write down on a piece of paper what we wanted from God in the coming year. The thought intrigued me—like being granted three wishes from a magic genie.

What do I want?… What do I want?… What DO I want? I thought about firm thighs, hair that doesn't do that annoying ducktail thing in the back, and a doctor's prescription for chocolate three times a day. I wanted smooth sailing, a life without telemarketers, lots of lemon meringue pie, and a pink angora sweater. Somehow, those things didn't sound all that spiritual, so I jotted down the first thing that popped into my mind: *I want to know that I can trust God. REALLY trust him.* Then in case I decided to change my mind later, I didn't sign my name (so God wouldn't know it was from me).

It's not that I didn't trust God, it was more like…it was like…okay, I didn't trust him. But I didn't want him to know! What kind of child doesn't trust her Father? The kind who likes to trust herself, that's who. The kind who doesn't like her security pulled out from beneath her, who doesn't like surprises or putting her faith in something or Someone she can't see—or who won't fill her in on the details in advance.

I needed a do-over, but by then it was too late. From my pen to God's ears, my prayer had been prayed and the answer was on its way. The dot had turned blue.

The truth is, I had been fighting the Lord about having another baby. When I had come to faith in Christ, I already had Alison, our older daughter. I *had* to trust God with her life, but I didn't want to trust him with another child. To my thinking the world was too scary, and I was too afraid to bring another baby into it. But, well, you know how things go. The next thing I knew, I was tossing my cookies and digging out my maternity clothes from the back of the closet.

Actually, the news wasn't as bad as I thought it would be. In fact, when my pregnancy test came out positive, I was filled with an odd, peaceful sensation. *Could this be trust?* I wondered. It could've been, but it was probably a hormone rush and not the magic *Poof!* of Instant Trust that I had secretly hoped God would endow me with.

Still, for the next two weeks God let me revel in the notion that my prayer had been answered, that I'd received an everlasting dose of trust in him and now would never waver or falter. Clouds were fluffier; the sky was bluer; chocolate never tasted chocolatier. Barry was up for a promotion at work, my ducktail was growing out, and we were going to have another baby. All was well with my soul.

Then Barry appeared at the back fence of our apartment in the middle of the afternoon. He had a check in his hand. "I lost my job," he said.

The clouds went flat; the sky turned bleak. The hair on the nape of my neck returned to its natural ducklike point. And I knew that *this* also was the answer to the prayer I had prayed.

Do-over! Do-over! I've changed my mind; I don't want to trust you, Lord. Poor Barry. I didn't know how I would tell him that it was all my fault—that I had inadvertently asked God to wreak havoc on our tidy little shallow-faithed existence. Accidentally setting fire to kitchen towels he could excuse; locking myself out of the bathroom and busting a hole in the door he could understand. But causing him to be laid off at the exact time we needed his income (not to mention his health-insurance plan) because of a baby on the way? *That* he wouldn't exactly do a cha-cha over.

So I kept it to myself and set about to make everything right.

First I sat down with the calculator and a box of Saltines and calculated all our money sources to see how long Barry could go without another job before we'd be out on the street. I estimated we could last until the following Tuesday, or if we were extremely careful, until January. (This was September.) I reminded God that I trusted him to find Barry a job by then.

Then in a spirit of total trust, I phoned the health-insurance company to make sure the baby was still covered under Barry's health plan. As I listened to an instrumental version of "She's Havin' My Baby" while on hold, I took it as a sign from heaven that the answer was, of course, yes.

The answer was, of course, no. No job, no health coverage. Duh.

I reminded God once again that I trusted him—just in case he forgot that in seven months a squalling baby Kennedy would need paying for. He didn't answer except to remind me that "in quietness and trust is your strength" (Isaiah 30:15). And then the bills came in like a flood...and God said, *"Trust me."* And then I learned the baby was Rh positive (and I am Rh negative), which might cause complications...and God said, *"Trust me."*

And then our septic line flooded our apartment and ruined some of our things...and God said, *"Trust me."*

And Barry couldn't find a job in September, October, November, December...and God still said, *"Trust me."*

Then my imposed deadline came, and I reminded God once again that I said I would trust him until January, but after that Barry needed a job. Up until then he had been looking diligently every day but could not find a permanent, full-time job. Someone bigger than we were was invisibly calling all the shots.

February came and went. March came and went.

And then we got an April surprise. But before I tell you about it

(I like to leave the good stuff for last), let me go back and fill in the holes of my saga.

When I got off the phone with the insurance company the day Barry lost his job, I munched a few saltines to calm my nausea, then called my friend Becky. As I recall, Becky had wild red hair and an even wilder faith in Christ. She saw everything as a gift from heaven. I should've remembered that before I called her. What I wanted was someone to commiserate with me and to keep me company down in the doldrums. What I got was an earful of glee.

"What a wonderful opportunity to trust the Lord!" she squealed. (And she called herself my friend.)

"I'd rather lick soap," I told her.

She ignored my obvious plea for sympathy, then prayed, "Lord, show Nancy and Barry and their family that you are a God that can be trusted. That when they're on the other side of this situation, they won't be able to count all the ways you've taken care of them."

That turned out to be one of the most powerful prayers that had ever been prayed for me, and the months that followed became the hardest, best, most wonderfully awful time of our lives. I don't even know where to begin.

- Our family doctor offered his services at a reduced rate, then let us pay him "whenever."
- The apartment manager where we lived gave Barry maintenance work to do in exchange for our rent.
- Barry found enough temporary odd jobs to keep him busy and able to earn a little money.

- Just when things looked bleak—the grace period on the car payment was about to run out—we'd find an envelope of money or a check from our church stuffed in our mailbox.
- A woman I didn't know well backed up to our door, her pickup truck loaded with groceries, and filled my kitchen with food. I'll never forget six-year-old Alison's face as she cried, "Mom, this is just like Christmas!"
- A man delivered two twenty-five pound hams to my front door.
- A woman at church (whose brusqueness had always intimidated me) *told* me that I was to hand over all my bills and she would pay them.
- A woman in my Bible study put cash in my purse every week when I wasn't looking.
- Our Sunday-school class stocked our kitchen with food.
- Someone gave us a ticket to a cut-your-own Christmas tree lot.
- Someone else bought Alison Christmas gifts.

That's just a list of things that I can remember; I know there were lots more. God said, "Trust me," and then he proved himself trustworthy.

Now for the best part. By the end of March (with our baby due in April), we still didn't have a clue how we would pay the hospital. Then Barry got a call from his Air National Guard unit. They offered him a sixty-day active-duty assignment to England—one that just happened to be in April, which just happened to mean if the baby was born while he was gone, the air force would pay the hospital costs.

And that's what happened. On April 23, 1983, Laura Elizabeth Kennedy was born out of trust and without any complications. When she was a month old, Barry returned home, and a month later he found a permanent, full-time job.

Here's where I'm supposed to say, *and I've trusted God wholeheartedly ever since*, but I already told you I'd rather tell you the truth. Trusting is hard. I'm hoping it gets easier—I'm praying that it does. Maybe it's one of those "We won't be perfect until we get to heaven" deals. Or maybe it's like a muscle: The more we use it, the stronger it gets.

Or maybe it doesn't have anything to do with us at all. God is trustworthy whether we trust him or not. He will always do the kind, just, and loving thing for all of his children. He will never forsake them, never leave them hopeless.

Trusting on my part, then, brings freedom from worry and anxiety. As the hymn says, "'Tis so sweet to trust in Jesus, just to take him at his word; just to rest upon his promise; just to know, 'Thus saith the Lord.'" Knowing I don't have to fret over incidentals (like what I shall eat or wear or where I shall live) because I have a God who is trustworthy to provide what I need *is* sweet. And it gets sweeter as the years go by.

Still, next time someone asks me to write down what I want from God, I'm going to be prepared. Next time I'm going to ask for peace.

⚜

Father,
You have called yourself a refuge in times of trouble and have said you care for those who trust in you (Nahum 1:7). Thank you, Lord, for counting me among the ones you care for. Oh, for grace to trust you more! Amen.

THINK ON THESE THINGS

- Think of a time when you consciously put your trust in God for a particular situation. What did you think would happen? What actually did happen? How did God work in your situation to prove himself trustworthy?

- Read Psalm 37. List the consequences of fretting or worrying. Now list the benefits of trusting. Also note every promise of God in this psalm for believers. What other scriptures help you in the area of trusting the Lord?

- Memorize Proverbs 3:5-6. "Trust in the LORD with all your heart and lean not on your own understanding; in all your ways acknowledge him, and he will make your paths straight." What does it mean to "lean not on your own understanding"? What are you trusting in God for right now? Commit it to him, and don't forget to watch how he acts on your behalf.

- "If a man will resign himself in implicit trust to the Lord Jesus, he will find that he leads the wayfaring soul into the green pastures and beside the still waters, so that even when he goes through the dark valley of the shadow of some staggering episode, he will fear no evil. Nothing in life or death, time or eternity, can stagger a soul from the certainty of the Way, for one moment."—Oswald Chambers, *My Utmost for His Highest*

FOUR

I Never Met a Cookie I Didn't Fall in Love With

HELP ME WHEN I'M TEMPTED

Lead me not into temptation—
I can find it myself!
BUMPER STICKER

Some people say everyone has a soul mate somewhere out there. I happen to believe we can have several. After all, I do—all of them cookies.

I have loved each and every cookie I have ever met, ever since the time I was big enough to lick the front case window at my grandmother's bakery in Los Angeles. It was there I was introduced to delicate sugar cookies with maraschino cherries in the middle, sturdy nut bars, and giant, cakelike "moon cookies" with half chocolate, half white icing. But most of all I loved the chocolate-chip cookies. With my eyes as big as my hips, I'd watch as my grandmother took racks and racks of them out of her brick oven, hot and steamy and gooey. I'd snitch a few into my pocket, stuff a few in my mouth, and pile a bunch into a pink cookie box to take home with me.

Up until now, my undying devotion to cookies, especially chocolate-chip cookies, has known no end. *Give me Mrs. Fields's Chocolate Chunk Macadamia Nut cookies, or give me death!* (And give me a bigger pair of pants while you're at it.)

Therein lies the problem. As much as I love and adore cookies, which have reciprocated by attaching themselves permanently to my thighs, I'm afraid I've become, um, too big for my britches. The bod isn't what she used to be.

Now, I've been on hundreds of diets in my lifetime, and I've lost hundreds of pounds. Unfortunately I've also found them all—plus their relatives and friends—and if you ask me, it's getting too crowded in my clothes for all of us. Let's just say it's a strain, especially in the seams of my pants.

The other day I reached a breaking point. Actually it was the zipper on my jeans that reached the breaking point. I knew it was time. Despite our four-decade-long love affair, my beloved cookies had become the bane of my existence. It was time for us to part company and go our separate ways.

Sadly, forlornly, I bid them adieu and turned to my bag of mini carrot sticks for solace. However, my heart still yearned for the silky decadence of a chocolate morsel surrounded by buttery crunchiness. *A crumb, just a crumb.* I flipped through the pages of a magazine, fantasizing over the full-color photos of holiday cookies and remembering only the day before when I had eaten my last one (double chocolate mint chunk).

I closed the magazine and prayed, "Lord, lead me not into temptation. My spirit is willing, but this body of mine is so weak!"

My craving subsided for all of three minutes; then it returned. I kept repeating, "It's not a sin to be tempted," as I opened the magazine again and started reading some recipes, waiting for God to give me strength, power, and self-control as he led me not into cookie's snare. "It's not a sin to be tempted, it's not a sin to be tempted," I chanted as I sneaked a peak at the recipe for peanut-butter jumbles. *Mmmm, peanut-butter jumbles. Peanut-butter jumbles with chocolate chips. Mmmm.*

I closed my eyes and pictured a chocolate-chip peanut-butter jumble. I imagined the aroma and did my best to recall how it might taste, the whole time congratulating myself on not falling into temptation. Instead of being filled with cookies, I was filled with self-satisfaction. I felt invincible! I was going to beat this hold that cookies had on me—and lose a few pounds in the process.

The next few days were repeats of that first. In the morning I prayed that the Lord would help me slay this Cookie Monster. Then I spent the rest of the day fighting temptation by studying magazines and cookbook recipes—yet I didn't eat a single cookie (although I did sniff the magazine picture of the blonde brownie bars and lick a bit of brown sugar off the page of the cookbook).

Then came the big test—the Cookie Exchange.

I'd been invited to my friend's cookie party and had looked forward to it for weeks. However, things had changed. Wisdom told me if I didn't go, I could avoid the temptation to eat every cookie in sight, but the more I thought about it, the more sense it made that I should go. That it was *good* for me to go, to look temptation square in the eye and say, "Ha! Gimme your best shot—I'm ready for ya." Yes, I'd prayed for God to "lead me not," but I was confident that he would not let me be tempted beyond what I could bear, and that he would provide a way of escape so I could stand up under it (1 Corinthians 10:13). I actually owed it to him to prove himself God over my temptation.

Now, despite what some people might say, I'm not a complete idiot. I knew better than to make a batch of cookies from scratch to bring with me. I'd never hold up under that kind of overwhelming temptation. Instead I decided to buy a package of cookies from the market shelf. Factory-sealed for my protection.

A funny thing happened on my way into the store. I had every intention of going right to the packaged cookie aisle, but my shopping cart took a detour to the refrigerator section where they keep the tubes of cookie dough.

Don't go there, warned the Voice inside my head.

I told the Voice, *But I'm just going to look!* And that's all I did. I looked…then ran my fingers down the seam of the package…then read the list of ingredients…then closed my eyes and tried to imagine the texture of raw dough in my mouth and the degree of bittersweetness in the chocolate chunks. *It's not a sin to be tempted,* I informed the Voice (before it had a chance to tell me I should drop everything and run).

Thoughts of hot, chewy, gooey cookies, fresh from the oven—for my friends, of course—baked into my mind. *Just think how delighted everyone will be. I owe it to them. Anyone could buy a package of cookies.*

These would be almost like homemade. Besides, I don't have to eat any. This is strictly an altruistic gesture. I'm doing it for others.

Up to my elbows in thoughtfulness, I set out to bake. And just in case temptation should try to entice me, I prayed twice for the Lord to lead me not.

The first batch went in the oven without my tasting even one tiny bit. Unless you count the blob of dough that fell on the counter and the chocolate chunk that stuck to the spoon. But everyone knows that doesn't count. Neither do broken cookies (I had to eat three of those), nor burnt ones (two). Plus, as the conscientious friend that I am, I was practically *required* to sample a whole one to make sure they were edible for my friends. That left six cookies out of twelve.

The next batch I dropped on the floor. I *had* to eat those (after I brushed them off) because we have a terrible problem with ants, and I couldn't throw them in the trash.

The last batch produced six picture-perfect cookies. And four lop-sided ones, which everyone knows don't count either, so I ate them as well. The rest of the dough somehow ended up in my mouth, and it wasn't until I'd eaten it that I realized…well, that I'd eaten it. But accidental eating doesn't count as "real" eating anyway. In fact, none of my cookie eating qualified as real eating, so technically I didn't succumb to temptation.

Still, I only had thirteen cookies to bring to the Cookie Exchange, and I needed three dozen. By then I didn't have time to bake any more, even if I'd had another tube of dough. I only had enough time to change into a pair of drawstring pants, finish off the remaining cookies (because of the ant problem) and stop by the store for a package of cookies.

On the way to the cookie exchange, I once again prayed for God to "lead me not into temptation." I planned to sip ice water all night and simply enjoy the fellowship—and leave without a plate of cookies. No one would know about my little "episode." Besides, I could always start clean tomorrow.

The first part of the evening went without a hitch. I found a spot near the table with all the cookies on it. It was far enough away that I couldn't touch them, but close enough for me to smell them. Although I'd eaten enough cookies earlier to satisfy the sweet tooth of every past, present, and future human being on earth, I didn't want to miss anything new. *What if someone brought Russian tea cakes? I'd never forgive myself for not getting a taste of those.*

Several times during the evening friends tried getting me away from my seat to join the party, but it was as if nothing else existed except cookies, glorious cookies. Eventually I did move. Closer to the table (so I could rest my water glass). I sniffed; I imagined; I savored; I salivated. I named each cookie. Blessed them. Praised them. *But I did not eat them.*

When everyone had divided the cookies and I had filled the tin I brought (for my family, of course), I said good night and got into my car to return home, duly impressed with myself. I opened the tin of cookies and popped one into my mouth as a congratulatory token.

That's when the Voice inside my head spoke once again. *What are you doing, Child?*

"Mmmif? Mmmif doeffn't count—I'm in ffuh car."

Suddenly the food in my mouth didn't taste as good as it had a minute ago. I swallowed what seemed like a rock. "But eating cookies isn't a sin!" I cried.

Whether you eat or don't eat cookies isn't the issue. Your flagrant flirting with the very thing you asked me to help you avoid is what concerns me. Don't you know by now that when you flirt with temptation you flirt with death?

"Death by cookies?"

Death by sin, Child. The cookies aren't important, but your soul is.

The Voice, of course, was right. I started to say, "Then why did you tempt me?" but then I remembered the words of James: "God is impervious to evil, and puts evil in no one's way. The temptation to give in to evil comes from us and only us. We have no one to blame but the leering, seducing flare-up of our own lust. Lust gets pregnant, and has a baby: sin! Sin grows up to adulthood, and becomes a real killer" (James 1:13–15, MSG).

Whether it's the temptation to eat too many cookies, spend money recklessly, watch trashy talk shows, gossip, lie, or think about men other than my husband, God never brings about the temptation, but always, always, *always* provides a way out. However, he expects me to make use of it. He's not a magic genie; he's holy God.

By the time I arrived home that night, my cookie binge had taken its toll on me. I rolled out of the car with the mother of all bellyaches and staggered to my front door. "Don't let them serve cookies at my funeral," I gasped to my husband as I crawled past him in the hall on my way to my (death) bed.

I can't be certain, but I think I heard God chuckle that night as I drifted off to sleep. I think he said something about making a grave error when I expect him to supernaturally protect me when I purposely place myself in temptation's way, and to beware whenever I think I'm standing firm because that's when I'm probably headed for a fall. Or in my case, a bout of indigestion.

As far as cookies being my soul mate, I've reconsidered. I think I'll get a cat instead.

❦

Lord,

I know it's not a sin to be tempted, but it is a sin to dwell on it, imagine it, live it in my mind. Next thing I know I'm up to my eyeballs in it. I'm so easily swayed toward evil. Please, Lord, hold my hand tight and help me not to pull it loose and go my own way when I'm tempted. Thank you for being patient with me. Amen.

THINK ON THESE THINGS

- When you have been tempted, what are some of the ways you have tried to overcome it? How have they succeeded (or failed)? Name some areas in which you are most tempted. What are some ways of escape you can use? What is the value of planning ahead for these times?

- According to James 1:13-14, where does temptation originate? What is its end result? Genesis 3 gives the account of the world's first-ever temptation and sin. What were the serpent's tactics?

How are they the same/different today? What was Eve's response? What should she have done differently?

• What hope do you find in Hebrews 4:14-16 for when you are tempted?

• "Temptation and testing are two sides of the same coin. Satan uses an occasion or a person to tempt us to fall; God uses the same to try us and make us stronger."—Ruth Bell Graham, *Women's Devotional Bible*

FIVE

Have Mine Own Way, Lord

HELP ME KNOW
AND DO YOUR WILL

The sweetest lesson I have learned in God's school
is to let the Lord choose for me.

UNKNOWN

I think I was in high school the first time I heard someone tell me, "God has a plan for your life." I don't remember who said it, but I do remember replying, "That's nice, but I have a plan of my own, thank you."

Basically my plan was simple: do what I want, when I want, with whom I want. I wanted to be my own judge of which books and magazines I should or shouldn't read, have the freedom to watch any movie or TV program that struck my fancy, eat lemon pie for breakfast and pancakes for dinner eight nights in a row. I wanted to blame-shift and finger-point with impunity, gossip freely with my neighbors, drive over the speed limit, and earn lots and lots of money. And spend it entirely the way I chose. When I grew old, I would play mah-jongg, interfere in my children's lives, go out with all my cronies for the Senior's Early Bird $4.99 Special, then bring home extra biscuits to feed the birds. Maybe get a face-lift or liposuction. Definitely get a big-screen TV and a *real* leather recliner. And be really cranky whenever I wanted just because I was old.

Doing things God's way didn't have the same appeal as looking out for number one while I was young or mowing people down with my cane and walker when I grew old. Besides, everybody knows as soon as you surrender your will to the will of God he packs you off to the Congo, where you spend the rest of your life teaching cannibals not to eat you. I didn't want to go to Africa, and I didn't want to be a missionary. Case closed. Leave me alone.

But God had a plan for my life, and since he runs the universe, his plan won out over mine. So when he called me into a relationship with himself, I found myself on my knees in surrender—and also in terror. *I'd prayed the prayer.* Before I could take it back, I'd uttered the life-changing words, "Almighty Lord, may your will be mine!" Then I waited for my Day of Reckoning. *Africa, here I come.*

I remember walking around for days after that, covering my head with my arms, waiting for the so-called bomb to drop. Every ring of the phone, every knock on the door caused my heart to pound and my knees to buckle. I didn't know what God had planned for me. Despite the words from Jeremiah 29:11 ("'For I know the plans I have for you,' declares the LORD, 'plans to prosper you and not to harm you, plans to give you hope and a future'"), I grieved over my soon-to-be loss of freedom—no more doing whatever I pleased. I kissed my dreams of a fun-filled life good-bye.

After a month of tiptoeing around, stockpiling books on jungle living, collecting recipes for deep-fried insects and Anaconda soufflé, after not hearing a single peep from heaven about trading my Lee jeans for a loincloth, I considered that maybe God *didn't* want to send me to Africa. But if not Africa, then where? If not a life as a missionary, then what? As a new Christian, I didn't have a clue how to determine God's will for my life.

Unfortunately neither did some of the people I asked.

I remember one woman who took me under her wing. She had black, curly hair and used the word "ravishing" a lot. She'd close her eyes and say things like, "Holy, great God, show this child your way," and then demand silence as we waited for a sign. She believed God has only *one* plan for each of his children's lives, and if we miss it, then we miss out on his blessings forever and ever. She also believed finding God's will was like looking for a needle in a haystack, that it was somehow mysteriously hidden from us and we had to constantly be on guard in case we should blink and miss it. She prayed agonizingly over every decision she made. *(Lord, should I eat bran flakes or scrambled eggs for breakfast? My blue sweater or the pink one?)* I learned early on not to get in line behind her at a potluck supper.

Fortunately it was God's will that this woman move to Arizona, where she could witness "ravishing desert sunsets." I'd only spent a few weeks with her, but by the time she left, I was wracked with doubts about my life. I had a hunch the Lord gives us free reign to choose our own breakfast cereal, but as for the rest of our lives, I wasn't so sure.

What did God want me to do? I continued praying fervently and searching for a sign. All I saw were Golden Arches and billboards for mental-health clinics. The biggies in my life—marriage and family—were already taken care of since I already had them when God called me, and I knew 1 Corinthians 7:20 says we're to remain in the situation we're in when God calls us. But what about a job? A ministry? Surely God had more for me to do than cook chicken, wash socks, and wipe noses.

As I prayed and searched for signs, I also searched the scriptures. At that time I didn't know how to study the Bible, so I used the method R. C. Sproul calls "luckydipping." Actually it's quite popular with many Christians. As you ask God for guidance, you let your Bible fall open to wherever it happens to open. Then with eyes shut, you "dip" your finger onto the page, and *voilà!* there's your divine answer.

I tried it several times. The first time I landed on "I have become a brother of jackals" (Job 30:29). The second try landed me on "This is my sickness, and I must endure it" (Jeremiah 10:19). The third time I landed on "He lived with the wild donkeys and ate grass like cattle" (Daniel 5:21).

I didn't try a fourth time. Instead I read of an opening for a volunteer counselor at the local Crisis Pregnancy Center. I decided since they needed someone and I found out about it, it must be God's will that I take the job. That I didn't want to do it, that I hated every minute of it and dreaded going each Monday morning, only "proved" to me that it must be God's will. *Surely he requires sacrifice and tension headaches and upset stomachs,* I reasoned. My family didn't like my going, mainly because I was a grouch on the days I spent at the center. *More proof,* I thought. *Everyone who does God's will suffers persecution.*

Eventually I was "fired" from my volunteer position. The director suggested perhaps my particular gifts could be used somewhere else, which I took as a kind way of saying, "You stink." Then she gave me the task of forming an auxiliary and organizing several fund-raisers for the center.

I raced home, excited beyond my wildest dreams and bursting with ideas for rummage sales and other stuff. She made me president, and I couldn't wait to tell my family. That the job required organization and delegation skills, a keen mind for details, and leadership qualities (of which I have none) didn't even register. All I knew was that I thought I had discovered God's will for my life.

My first duty as president was to gather people together for a meeting to talk about whatever it is presidents are supposed to talk about to their people. I hadn't a clue. All I'm good at is showing up.

So I did. I showed up and waited for the meeting to start. When I realized I had to start it, I fumbled through until it was finally time to eat cookies and adjourn. (*That* I can do too.) Someone suggested we have a rummage sale; someone else appointed chairpeople. I volunteered to show up.

Only because God has pity on innocents and fools, not because of my reluctant leadership, the rummage sale was a success. Afterward, however, I wrote a letter to everyone who had been involved, encouraging and commending them as a group and as individuals. I didn't even type it and the handwriting was crooked, but everyone who read it commented on how it had touched them. Someone suggested I write a newsletter for the center. Someone else suggested I publish professionally.

I hadn't really considered a writing career; I just liked to write stuff. But I didn't just *like* it, I loved it. I still do. I love every aspect of forming thoughts into words and arranging them on paper. To me it's like what the 1924 British Olympic athlete Eric Liddell said about running in the movie *Chariots of Fire*: "When I run, I feel God's pleasure." When I write, I feel God's pleasure.

Could that be God's will for me?

In his book *The Great House of God,* author Max Lucado offers these guidelines for determining God's will: Consider the godly counsel of others, read the Word of God, remain in close relationship with the Lord, and "heed the fire within." For me, the fire within, the passion and the gifts God has given me, involves communicating and encouraging. I'm a cheerleader for the Lord. I have no fire for administration, and I'm not a planner or an idea person, but give me a tape recorder, a pen, and a blank piece of paper, and I will find a story to tell, whether it's mine or someone else's. Chances are, writing is God's will for my life.

On the other hand, not everything I love doing is God's will for me. I remember a home sewing job I had for a few years. Although I love sewing, after a while I knew the Lord wanted me to give it up. Thinking about what I had to do, doing it, or preparing for the next day's work consumed almost all of my days—*seven days a week, for ten dollars a day.* I fought God's will for nearly a year because I didn't want to stop doing what I loved, and I thought I needed the money. Finally I prayed, *"Lord, I DON'T want to quit this job—I'm afraid to quit. But if you change my heart, I'll do it."*

The very next day I wanted to quit that job more than anything. Almost immediately after I did, opportunities to write professionally came at me from all directions. My puny sewing job had only been holding me back from something far greater. Ten years later I'm still amazed that it would be the Lord's will for me to do what I love.

For the most part, finding God's will for my life isn't a mystery. He opens doors; he closes them. He gives me other Christians and his Word to provide counsel. He gives me gifts and talents and the opportunities to use them. He works in me "to will and to act according his good purpose" (Philippians 2:13). He changes my will to conform to his own.

As for my life in general, it's God's will that I love my neighbor, live ethically, confess my sins, remain in fellowship with him, and do everything to his glory. I'm to keep myself sexually pure within my marriage and not lie, cheat, or steal. The list goes on. But in the specifics of my life—what I eat or where I go on my vacation—I believe I have unbridled freedom within the boundaries of Scripture.

What about God's will for my future? If I knew that, I'd be God. I might very well go to Africa someday. Or I might write about someone else who has gone. Until then I'll continue doing what I'm doing: driving my daughter to school in the mornings, vacuuming the living room, watering the dry patch of grass out back, remaining close to the Father, reading his Word, heeding the fire he places within me. Trusting that he wants to reveal his will to me.

And praying that his will always will be mine.

❧

Father,
I confess that I often just don't know what I should do. Or if I know, I often don't want to do it. Yet your plans are always best, and your will

for my life is always so much greater than I could ever hope for or imagine. It may not always be easy, but it always brings joy—even in pain and sorrow. Thank you that you don't keep your will for my life hidden. Help me to seek it with all my heart, that I may glorify you always. Amen.

THINK ON THESE THINGS

- What means has God given us to determine his will for our lives? How would you respond to someone who says God has only one perfect (spouse, career, ministry) for each of us? What is your position? What scriptures support your view?

- If God is sovereign and nothing happens outside of his will, what about "mistakes"? Think of the church planter who, after much prayer and seeking after the Lord, starts a church, only to have it fail after two years. Or think of a time in your life when you thought you were doing God's will but it turned out to be a "mistake." Looking back, what did you learn from it? How might this fit in with God's will for your life?

- Romans 12:4-8 talks about spiritual gifts within the body of Christ. What are they and how can you determine what your gifts are? What are you doing to exercise your gifts? Pray and ask God to open up opportunities for you to "heed the fire within." Don't forget to thank him!

- "If we want God to guide us…first we must be willing to think. It is false piety, super-supernaturalism of an unhealthy pernicious sort that demands inward impressions with no rational base, and declines to heed the constant biblical summons to consider. God made us thinking beings, and he guides our minds as we think things out in his presence."—James Packer, *Your Father Loves You*

SIX

I'm Okay; He Could Use a Major Personality Overhaul

HELP ME CHANGE

Changing a tire is a lot easier than changing your husband.
A wedding ring makes a lousy lug wrench.

DIANA JORDAN

One of the funniest books I've ever read is called, *"I Love Him, But…"* In it Merry Bloch Jones asked over two hundred women across America to fill in the blank with what drove them crazy about their husbands. Here's what some of them said:

I love him, but…he wears wingtips and black socks. Even in hot weather, with shorts. Like a refugee from an accounting firm.

I love him, but…he asks blunt questions. "Pregnant, Sue?" "Dyed your hair, Wanda?"

I love him, but…he trims his chest hair…rewashes the dishes I wash…insists that I scoop ice cream out so it's level…loves horse art.

I love him, but…he can never remember our PIN number at the bank machine. It's our anniversary date!

In my twenty-four years of marriage to Barry, I could fill in a few blanks of my own. I love him, but…we can't leave for a trip without his checking *all* the appliances in the house and asking me a thousand times if I turned the stove off. Then when we're five miles out of town, we have to turn back, "Just in case you forgot to lock the front door."

I love him, but…when he talks to somebody on the phone long-distance he yells—like his friend Danny in Pennsylvania can't hear him unless he shouts.

I love him, but…when he's working out in the yard, he'll grab my head and stick it under his armpit. To him, that's a sign of affection.

I love my husband, but…he doesn't understand my tears, can't satisfy the deepest desires of my heart, and won't ever be who I think he should be. Not only that, despite my best efforts and most fervent prayers, I can't change him.

Of course, it took me a long time to learn that.

In my book *Honey, They're Playing Our Song,* I begin by saying, "My husband Barry and I met, got married, and fell in love—in that order." We did what every parent fears their children will do: rush blindly into the most sacred and important decision of their lives and base it solely on physical chemistry. I liked him because he was the only guy who ever bought me ice skates. He liked me because of my then-red hair, my green eyes, and the way I walked.

We got married after knowing each other only three months. Well, we sort of knew each other. We didn't really get to know each other until months after the cheesy ceremony at the local Justice of the Peace's office. If I had doubts beforehand (which I did), by the time it was too late, I'd acquired a severe case of buyer's remorse.

But God. My two favorite words! But God drew me unto himself, gave me a new heart, and began within me a process of change, which of course I tried to pass on to my husband. It made perfect sense. Since God was changing me, Barry should change too, right? God knew he needed it more than I did.

I don't remember the exact words, but I prayed something like, "Lord, I don't want to mention any names, but some people in this marriage need changing. Some people aren't loving the other person the way the Bible says, and some people are quite selfish in their dealings with the other. Some people hog the remote and leave used tissues on the dresser and won't wear anything unless it looks as if it were rubbed on a cheese grater first. Some people need to be more understanding and giving and caring. I'll do whatever I can to help, Lord, because you know how some people are. Amen."

I prayed, then sat back and waited for the changin' to begin. I loved my husband, but...he fell so far short of what a husband should be. He needed to be shown what it means to be full of grace and mercy for another human being, forgiving, contrite, and truly humble. He needed to be shown that God could turn a self-centered, arrogant sinner into an others-centered servant.

I never dreamed the Lord would use me as his show-and-tell project.

Truthfully, I didn't think I was all that bad. Sure, I needed a few tweaks here and there, but I considered myself basically okay. Barry, on the other hand...

Now comes the hard part: trying to condense over a decade of my efforts to "help" God change my husband and change our marriage. Where do I even begin?

How about wanting him to be sensitive like Phil Donahue, charming like James Bond, chic like John Travolta in *Saturday Night Fever*— basically, someone other than himself? I wanted romance. I wanted witty repartee and snappy banter. I wanted life to be a 007 movie with Barry as leading man, suave and debonair. Or at least with his hair combed at all times. He could keep his easygoing nature, his intense work ethic, and strong sense of responsibility...and the crinkly smile lines around his brown eyes, and his well-developed arm muscles (hubba, hubba). But the rest of him needed a major overhaul.

Unfortunately, the harder I tried the do-it-myself approach, the harder he resisted. I couldn't understand it. I was only trying to help. We'd have conversations like this:

"Barry, you really should wear a sports coat more often."

"You really should leave me alone and get yourself a Ken doll to dress up."

Or this:

"Barry, why don't you ever write me a love poem?"

"Why don't you ever write me a check?"

I complained to all my friends about all his faults (and they'd complain about their own husbands). But after a while, something didn't feel right. I started feeling disloyal to Barry. I overheard my former pastor's wife tell someone, "After listening to the way some women tear down their husbands, by the time I meet the guys, I already hate them."

That comment has stayed with me, and back then it served as a turning point in my life. I began to look at the things I said *to* Barry and *about* him. To tell you the truth, I was ashamed. I was the one who needed changing.

Again, how do I begin to condense the next decade of the changes God has made in me? To begin with, I stopped hounding Barry about what he wore, where he put (or didn't put) his drinking glass, and all the other things that irritated the daylights out of me. Instead I became a student of my husband. Ephesians 5:33 instructs wives to respect their husbands. *The Amplified Bible* says it this way: "Let the wife see that she respects and reverences her husband [that she notices him, regards him, honors him, prefers him, venerates, and esteems him; and that she defers to him, praises him, and loves and admires him exceedingly]." Whew! That's a tall order, one that I can't fill on my own, but I *can* do it through Christ, who gives me strength (Philippians 4:13).

Over the years I've learned that my husband, like most men, needs admiration and respect above anything else. And loyalty. In his book *For Better or for Best,* Gary Smalley tells wives that admiration is a choice. He writes, "Your husband might irritate you, belittle you, offend you, ignore you, or basically nauseate you, but admiration looks beyond what he does to who he is. It's unconditional." He adds this word of encouragement (and warning): "Men tend to gravitate toward those who admire them."

As I write this, I'm having a hard time trying to dredge up memories of all the things that irritated me about Barry back then—that's how much God has changed me. I think my major complaint wasn't so much what he did as what he didn't do. I expected him to do for me what only the Lord can do. Then when he failed, I resented him for it. My resentment translated to a lack of admiration for him, which caused him not to want to be around me, which caused me to resent him even more, which caused...

Around the same time I overheard my pastor's wife's comment, I had an epiphany. How do you explain a work of the Holy Spirit? A scripture in Isaiah leaped off the pages of my Bible and wormed its way into my heart: "For your Maker is your husband" (54:5). I saw that the Almighty was my true husband—the only one who could utterly and completely satisfy every longing I had—and that he had given me Barry to love, honor, cherish, and obey. I was to serve rather than be served, whether he changed or not. Whether our marriage changed or not.

I think the key to change is surrender. I give up my rights to happiness (which truly aren't rights at all). I give up my expectations of happily ever after and moonlit walks on the beach and roses for no apparent reason. I surrender wanting to control my destiny, manipulate my surroundings, play puppeteer with those around me. I give up. And God says, *"You didn't have control anyway, Child."*

But God does have control, and by his Spirit he gives me the power to control my tongue, my actions, and my daydream fantasies. He says to us all, "Be good wives to your husbands, responsive to their needs." As for husbands who are indifferent or even hostile to the Word of God, "[They] will be captivated by your life of holy beauty" (1 Peter

3:1-2, MSG). That's not a guarantee, but God knows men well enough to know what makes them tick.

Oh, by the way: The most amazing thing occurred about six months after I decided God was God and I was not. Barry took me aside and said, "You know, you've changed. You're nice to me. You like me now."

Who says my husband's not a poet?

Lord,

I can change my attitudes, I can change my actions, but only you can change my heart of stone. Sometimes I look in the mirror, and I don't even recognize who I am now. Thank you for changing me and making me into a whole new creation. Keep at it, Lord, for I still have a long way to go. Amen.

THINK ON THESE THINGS

- If you could change anything about your life, what would it be and why? If you haven't already, surrender these areas of desired change to God. Are there specific steps you need to take to start you in the right direction? What are they?

- In 2 Corinthians 5:17, Paul writes, "Therefore, if anyone is in Christ, he is a new creation; the old has gone, the new has come!"

In thinking about your life, contrast your old ways with the evidence of being a new creation. Thank God for the work he's done in you. (If you have never submitted yourself to Christ, why not take the opportunity to do it now? Then you, too, will be a new creation.)

• Personalize Ezekiel 36:25-27 by inserting your name or the name of someone on your prayer list and making it your prayer. Other scriptures to use as prayers include: Isaiah 64:8; Ephesians 4:22-24; 2 Corinthians 3:18; Psalm 139:23-24.

• "The hope of the Christian is far deeper than a change in someone else.... Our responsibility is to respond to life's events in a manner intended to please the Lord, not to change our spouses into what we want."—Larry Crabb, *The Marriage Builder*

❧

Don't Just Do Something, Sit There!

HELP ME WAIT

I coulda had a V8!

JUICE AD

My soul is in anguish. How long, O Lord, how long? I knew just how King David felt when he wrote that psalm. My soul was also in anguish. Actually, it was my shin. I was eleven years old, and I had been waiting my *entire life* to shave my legs. My mom said I needed to wait, but what do moms know? I had a forest growing on my lower limbs that needed razing. Now. Not when I was "old enough," which is at best an arbitrary concept. Of course, when you're eleven, you don't use words like "arbitrary." You lie across your bed and sob because life isn't fair and your mom is mean, and you plot to shave your legs anyway.

Which I did. While visions of smoothness danced in my head, I sneaked my dad's razor into the bathroom, lathered up my legs, and took one long, flesh-cutting swipe—and bled like crazy all over the bathroom for the next hour and a half. Mom found out (a pile of crimson-stained bath towels stuffed in a closet is always a dead give-away) and was *not* pleased. Since selective memory prohibits me from remembering what happened next, I'm guessing that Mom applied something we called "burny-burny" on my self-inflicted wound, prob-ably using an extra dose on my leg as part of this painful lesson. After that I most likely ended up where I began, sobbing on my bed because life isn't fair and you have to wait for stuff you want *right now*.

Afterward Mom probably peeked her head in my room and said something like, "Waiting builds character." However, when you're eleven years old, you don't want character, you want smooth legs.

Now here would be a good place to say I learned my lesson, but you've been eleven yourself, and you know that's not likely. I could tell you that once I came to faith in Christ I put off disregarding any and all directives to wait and never took matters into my own hands ever again. But I suppose by now you know that's not true either. And I promised I'd tell you the truth.

The truth is, often I'm still an eleven-year-old lying across my bed, sobbing that life isn't fair. The truth is, since coming to faith in Christ, waiting is often a whole lot harder because, by its very nature, living in faith involves a lot of waiting. Otherwise it wouldn't be faith.

That doesn't mean I like it. "The trouble is," said New England preacher Phillips Brooks in the late 1800s, "I'm in a hurry, but God isn't." Yes, yes, yes. So true, so true. And that brings me to my prayer.

How long, O Lord, how long? I want patience—and I want it
NOW. I want a crash course in knowing you, plus instant knowl-
edge and freeze-dried "just add water" wisdom. I could use imme-
diate strength of character and on-the-spot holiness. How long,
O Lord, how long? If it's true that they who wait upon you will
renew their strength, then help me wait, Lord. Help me wait.
ASAP.

I should have known God would answer a petition to "Help me wait" with long intervals of silence, prayers marked "return to sender," and seeming nonexistence on his part. But I was naive enough to think he'd give me what I wanted, when and how I wanted it, just because I said I was willing to wait for it. I know that's not even logical, but it's what I thought. Actually, I just hoped God would think I was sincere. I didn't really want to wait for anything. Especially one particular thing, which I'll tell you about in a little bit.

Funny thing about God: He knows what he's doing and doesn't need my help to do anything. He also knows that when I take matters into my own hands and try to speed things along, I just make things worse and am left with a mess, saying, "I wish I would've waited on God!" Of course it's taken me twenty years to figure that one out. From the start I should've listened to the prophet Habakkuk, who said, "The LORD is in his holy temple; let all the earth be silent before him" (2:20). Or Peter, who said, "The Lord is not slow in keeping his promise" (2 Peter 3:9). Or Solomon, who wrote, "There is a time for everything, and a season for every activity under heaven" (Ecclesiastes 3:1). Or even the radio DJ, who put it another way: "God never says, 'Oops.'"

That brings me to the "one thing" I want to tell you about. It involves something I'm waiting for eagerly. Desperately at times. I'm waiting for my dearest friend to fall in love with Jesus. For us to pray together and know genuine spiritual oneness. I want it so bad that at times I can taste it. Do you know what that's like? Of course you do. Everyone has *someone* they're praying for.

I told you in the last chapter about wanting to change my husband. But I didn't tell you about being a new believer and winning the prize for Most Obnoxious Sharer of the Gospel with One's Spouse. (Not really, but if there had been a prize, I would've won it.) Poor Barry. *He* wins the prize for grace under pressure as I lived out my faith before him as obnoxiously as I could. I tried *everything*. Preaching, teaching, screeching. Finger pointing into his chest and describing an eternity of "weeping and wailing and gnashing of teeth." (I may have even demonstrated the teeth-gnashing part.)

I'd blast my Christian music out the window when he worked on the car, and I always made sure there was an open Bible on the back of the toilet. And every Sunday morning I'd beg and plead with him to go to church with me. Then when he wouldn't, I'd sulk and try my hardest to make him sorry. He was sorry all right—sorry he married me. He even told me once, "I'd leave you if I could afford it." I just chalked it up to being persecuted for righteousness' sake.

Yet with every nagging word, I was eleven years old again, scraping my own skin. Taking matters into my own hands and bleeding all over the floor, then railing against heaven because life's not fair and I wanted what I wanted, when I wanted it.

Then something unexpected happened.

I'd been reading a book about intercessory prayer and had an "aha!" moment. I said, "That's it! I'm going to wait on the Lord and pray for Barry for the next eighty years, if that's what it takes. I'll just wait and pray. Period."

I hope you're not expecting me to say that was the day I ceased all my manipulation. Much of it, but not all. Something did happen on that day, however. That was the day I began to consider that God just might know what he's doing after all. That he didn't need my "help." That he had a plan and a grand design for me as well as for Barry, and that the best way to accomplish it was through our being spiritually mismatched. Twenty years later I *know* he knows. Back then it was a radical concept.

Also back then I never dreamed my decision to "just wait and pray" would take so long (although I did say I'd pray for the next eighty years). You want to know the truth? I've come to value this waiting time. It's made me who I am and enabled me to offer hope to others in waiting. It's given me a message and a voice. To me and you God says, "I have not abandoned you in your waiting but am strengthening you. I have not been cruel, but kind."

Currently I'm waiting for my house to sell. I'm waiting for my younger daughter to sort out her doubts concerning Christ. I'm waiting for many things, but mostly I'm waiting on the Lord, watching for him to move and work, trusting that he will perfect everything that concerns me, when he wants it done.

"Be still before the LORD and wait patiently for him," wrote the psalmist (Psalm 37:7). I'm no theologian, but I think the measure of your ability to wait patiently is proportionate to the measure of your belief in the absolute sovereignty of God. Here's how I see it: God is God. He knows what he wants to do, when he wants to do it. It's his universe, and he can do with it as he pleases. It pleased him to wait until I was twenty-three to call me into a relationship with himself. For another person his plan might be to wait until he or she is fifty-three or seventy-three…or one hundred and three. There is a time and a season for everything under heaven. It's my job to be still and wait—for the *Lord* and not for what I want him to do for me.

That's the secret. "We yearn for this, we ache for that, and concentrate on what we want and not on God," says author Gladys Hunt in the *Women's Devotional Bible*. But the Bible tells us to wait *on the Lord*. Besides, it's in the waiting that we receive some of our greatest blessings. I never would have known that I *can* endure with hope and persevere with patience—and have joy!—unless I had been made to wait.

"Because God is in control, we can be patient," writes Jim Long in *Campus Life* magazine. "Because God loves us, we can relax. Because God's wisdom is flawless, we can wait."[1]

Because we wait for God, we wait for what's best.

⚭

Lord,
Waiting is so hard, yet when I try to make things happen, I just make everything worse. Remind me, Lord, that you are God and I am not. I know this is one prayer I won't have to wait long for you to answer. Amen.

THINK ON THESE THINGS

- What are some things you're waiting for and praying about? How is waiting on the Lord different from waiting for God to answer your prayer? Be honest. What if your prayer will never be answered the way you want it to be answered? How would that affect your faith?

- Because Abraham and Sarah took matters into their own hands concerning God's promise of descendants, they produced two opposing nations that are still at war with one another. Can you recall a time when you tried to "help" God fulfill his promises? What was the result? Some scriptures that talk about waiting on the Lord include Psalm 27:14, Psalm 130:5-6, and Isaiah 40:31 (NKJV). Write them down and memorize them for the next time you're tempted to "help" God.

- Read Romans 8:18-39. As you grapple with what you're waiting for, what hope do you find in this passage for your situation? List every pertinent thought, and then use the list to give thanks to God for all he is doing for you while you wait for him.

- "God wants us to enjoy where we are, on the way to where we're going. We might as well learn to wait well because it is a fact of life—and we'll spend a lot of time being miserable if we don't."— Joyce Meyer

---

[1] Jim Long, "Give Me Patience...Now!" *Campus Life,* March-April 1998.

❦

EIGHT

"Mom, Why Can't I Get a Tattoo?"

HELP ME PERSEVERE

Diamonds are nothing more than chunks of coal that stuck to their jobs.

MALCOM FORBES

Few people know this about me, but I'm a long-distance runner. In my dreams. In the daytime I have short, stumpy legs, but at 3 A.M., I'm long and lean. Like a cheetah. I have a recurring dream: As the theme song from *Chariots of Fire* plays in the background, I'm gliding down a track, one graceful, slow-motion stride at a time. My heart pounds; my breathing is steady. I'm doing it; I'm pushing; I'm making it. The crowd of witnesses roars, cheering me on. I'm feeling confident, strong, invincible.

Then just as I'm about to reach the end, my younger daughter appears out of nowhere and grabs my arm. "Mom," she pleads, "if I pay for it myself, *then* can I dye the front of my hair blue?"

With that, I lose both my concentration and my balance, trip over my shoelace, do a somersault into the dust, hit a tree, scrape my elbow, and bite my tongue. As all the other runners pass me by, I'm left wounded and defeated, eating dirt. I curl up into a fetal position and ponder the line of ants marching up my arm when I hear a voice from above: "Can I, Mom? Can I?"

That's usually the point in my dream where I wake up and vow never to eat chili-cheese hot dogs right before bed. That's also the point where I start looking for the escape clause in my motherhood contract. *There's got to be a sanity exception!*

My friend Sue says raising a teenage daughter is like Chinese water torture: a constant *drip, drip, drip* on the forehead until you eventually go insane. Between the two of us, we're almost there. *Drip, drip, drip.* Actually, insanity doesn't sound too bad—they put you in a nice sanitarium and take away sharp instruments and let you glue macaroni on soup cans and spray paint them gold. But then your daughter comes to visit and asks, "Well, if I can't dye my hair blue, can I at least get a tattoo?" *Drip, drip, drip.*

The other day Laura asked about piercing her eyebrow. No wait— she didn't *ask;* she *campaigned.* She handed me seven pages of documented research from the Internet, complete with a list of thirty-five Reasons to Say Yes ("It will not harm any living creature." "I won't wear the eyebrow ring to any formal occasion." "It is better than piercing my tongue.") I remained calm for all of twenty minutes as she followed me up and down the aisles of the market. I had almost made it to the last aisle when her "It's the same as your dying your hair" set me off. I was back in my dream, licking the dust. But this time—in real life—I didn't curl up in a fetal position to contemplate insects. This time I grabbed the nearest thing (a can of Pringles) and threw it. In the market. In front of God and my neighbors and the potato-chip guy stocking the shelves and everybody. It exploded all over the place. *I* exploded all over the place, flailing my arms and emitting guttural sounds. Some woman tiptoed past me and whispered to her child in the basket, "That's what people do who don't know Jesus, honey."

It was not my most shining hour.

Somehow I cleaned up my mess (as Laura nonchalantly edged her way over to the magazine rack), gathered up my groceries, paid for them, and answered three inquiries as to whether someone should be called to come and get me.

When I got home, I called my mother. She's usually good for a "you poor baby" or two. Not this time. This time she reminded me of my own relentless two-year campaign, starting in fourth grade, to wear stockings. "Just suck it in and drive on," she told me.

Or in other words, persevere.

The problem is, I prayed for perseverance once. I thought it was a good idea at the time. I'd been studying the book of Hebrews where it says to "run with perseverance the race marked out for us" (12:1). At the time all I could picture was my crossing a finish line in triumph, my fists in the air and a medal around my neck. *Yes, I want that!* I remember thinking, *I want to hear the roar of the crowd and feel the sweat on my arms. I want to finish—I want to win!*

So I prayed for perseverance. Instead I got a daughter who wants a tattoo.

Of course she didn't always want a tattoo. Or her eyebrow pierced. When she was younger, she used to concoct Barbie Water-Theme Parks in the kitchen by hanging colanders from the ceiling and pouring water into them and making her Barbie dolls slide down cookie sheets. Once she mixed blue food coloring into a jar of mayonnaise, and another time she wrote "I LOv YU Mom" on her door in permanent marker.

Laura doesn't enter a room; she pirouettes in. She watches the Weather Channel. She has two beds in her room, yet she prefers to sleep on the floor. She eats everything from a bowl, never a plate. She wears bright orange shoes and paints her fingernails black, carries a Barbie lunchbox as a purse, and wears a Crayola backpack—and she never uses slang.

Some days she says she isn't interested in God anymore. Some days she wants to be a Buddhist; other days she wants to go on a missions trip…or maybe live with a bunch of people in a "skanky" apartment and work in a music store part-time. Or maybe get a scholarship to a Christian college. Her taste in music is loud, her friends sport turquoise or magenta hair (the boys, not the girls), and some of them have places on their body pierced that ought not be pierced. At fifteen she wants to hop on a bus and travel to Seattle.

The kid drives me crazy.

And I think she's the answer to my prayer.

"Consider it a sheer gift, friends, when tests and challenges come at you from all sides," writes James. "You know that under pressure, your faith-life is forced into the open and shows its true colors. So don't try to get out of anything prematurely. Let it do its work so you become mature and well-developed, not deficient in any way" (James 1:2-3, MSG).

As the late Gilda Radner used to say, "It's always something." Something that either breaks our hearts and makes us want to quit—a debilitating illness, an unbelieving spouse. Or something that's merely an irritant, like an intruding relative or a child who never seems to lose steam in her attempt to wear you down. *It's always something.*

Sometimes it's a lot of somethings coming from all sides, forcing your faith-life into the open, revealing its true colors. That's when the temptation to quit is most enticing.

When the laundry multiplies, and the bank account doesn't.

When your children know only one speed: turbo.

When you try to share your faith and nobody cares.

And you find marijuana in your child's room.

And it's too much of a hassle to get everyone to church on Sunday.

When you read of the slaughter of believers around the world.

And you discover bisexuality is the in thing at the local high school.

And they just opened an abortion clinic in your town.

When you start to think, "Afternoon talk shows aren't *that* bad" and "Everybody else cheats on their income tax."

When you start imagining your life with a different spouse.

When you want to quit…

That's when God says, "Keep going. One more step. *Persevere.*" As someone once said, "It's the last step in a race that counts." Keep going. Don't quit. *Persevere.*

To be honest, I know the struggles I have with my daughter are minute and the struggles I have in my life in general are infinitesimal compared to many. I remember telling a friend, "If God gives us only what he knows we can handle, then he must think I'm a real wimp."

Even so, at times I'm tempted to quit, and I need the Lord's help to persevere.

And I will persevere.

Not because of anything I can or will ever do but because of God's tenacity. I love that word. It's a persistent, unrelenting holding on. A "love that will not let me go." When I trip and fall, when I'm licking dust and nursing bruises, God says, "One more step. *Persevere.*"

Harriet Beecher Stowe said, "When you get into a tight place and everything goes against you, till all seems as though you could not hold on a minute longer, never give up then, for that is just the place and time that the tide will turn."

I remember giving birth to Laura. My first daughter, Alison, had been a tiny thing, six and a half pounds, yet the doctor had said she was too big for my body. Then came Laura. Eight pounds, thirteen ounces. My labor was fairly short—six hours. However, it took another two hours to push, with every sinew in my body screaming to quit. But there was no turning back. The only thing I could do was persevere. With the end in sight, with the encouragement of others, with help from above, I persevered.

That's how I still feel about Laura. I will not quit on her. And God won't quit on me. The apostle Paul wrote, "We…rejoice in our sufferings, because we know that suffering produces perseverance; perseverance, character; and character, hope" (Romans 5:3-4). My hope is this: One day I *will* finish my race because God has promised to complete the work he began in me. I *will* endure, even if he has to carry me.

And Laura? I have confidence that she will endure too.

❧

Lord,

Perseverance sounds so good when things are going smoothly but not so good when all I want is to quit. Jesus, you, too, were tempted to quit. Yet "for the joy that was set before you" you endured the Cross. Help me to endure, to persevere just one more step, until I finish. Amen.

THINK ON THESE THINGS

- The Christian life is compared to running a race. What are some of the qualities a runner needs to run successfully? How do these qualities apply to the Christian life?

- Did you ever quit anything that you now regret? How would your life be different if you had stuck with it? Are you tempted to quit anything now? Why?

- James 1:2-3 (MSG) tells us to consider tests and challenges as gifts. How could you consider your current situation a gift?

- Hebrews 12:1 says to "throw off everything that hinders and the sin that so easily entangles, and…run with perseverance." What hinders and entangles you? Confess these areas of greatest stumbling, and ask God to help you keep running.

in his drive against slums, took every opportunity he
ell the people of New York about the evils they were
. It took a lot of telling, and he often became discouraged. When he did, he would go to watch a stonecutter hammer
away at a rock. The cutter might strike 100 blows without as
much as a crack showing. "Yet at the 101st blow, it will split in
two," Riis said. "I know it was not that blow that did it, but all
that had gone on before."

PART TWO

Make Me

Yet, O LORD, you are our Father.
We are the clay, you are the potter;
we are all the work of your hand.

ISAIAH 64:8

NINE

Memo to a Super Model: Eat Your Heart Out

MAKE ME BEAUTIFUL

Just standing around looking beautiful is so boring,
really boring, so boring.

MICHELLE PFEIFFER

I don't know about you, but just once I'd like to be described as a knockout instead of, "Well, she's got a *great* personality." You know how it goes: When God was passing out noses, I thought he said hoses, so I asked for a long one. I could add: When God was passing out hips, I thought he said lips, so I said, "Make mine round and full!" And when God was passing out hair, I thought he asked, "Where?" So still thinking of lips I answered, "On my face, of course."

When I get to heaven and finally see God, I have a question for him. Chin whiskers on women—*why?!* I remember as a teenager watching in horrifying revulsion as my mom plucked at stray hairs and shuddering as I thought, *What horrible sin did she commit that God would do this to her?* I vowed never, *ever* to do whatever it was she did. Unfortunately, it appears I did because now I'm the one plucking at stray chin whiskers— and my daughters are the ones watching me in revulsion. What's worse, I always manage to miss one, always long and black, always glaringly obvious, especially in broad daylight. Ah, but if anything, I am resourceful. That's why I've taken to cupping my chin in my hands in a pose of meditative contemplation. But just between you and me, if you ever see me outside and I look as if I'm deep in thought, you'll know—*chin whiskers.*

At the risk of sounding disrespectful, I think God made a mistake when he invented unwanted facial hair. I, for one, don't want it. And I've gone to great lengths over the years to get rid of it, beginning in junior-high school. Maybe it's a hormone thing, but around seventh grade I started sprouting a fuzzy caterpillar on my upper lip. Fortunately I discovered a miracle potion—cream hair remover. Just slap it on your face, let it sit for a few minutes, wash it off—*voilà!* No hair. Smooth as a baby's behind.

That lasted about three weeks. Then it burned the skin on my upper lip, leaving oozing, red blisters. Try going to junior high with that. Thankfully we had in our neighborhood a wonder-working Avon Lady, who came to the rescue with all kinds of lotions and cover-up stuff. But I still had bumps and ooze. In an unforgettable act of mercy, my mom let me stay home for a few days to recuperate and avoid facing certain death by humiliation.

I'm unhappy to say the hair grew back as thick and lush and unwanted as it had been originally. So I tried bleaching it. Still harsh on the skin but not as bad as the hair remover. The only problem was getting the bleach. I had to wait until my blond-haired mom retouched her dark roots. (Don't tell her I'm saying this or she'll kill me!) I'd sneak into the bathroom, squirt some of the purple goop in my hand, run to my room, smear it on my face, wait until it turned white and bubbly, then wipe it off.

That method lasted several years, until tragedy struck. *Mom let her hair grow dark.* Luckily, by then I had discovered tweezers. I'd spend hours plucking away and then rubbing my throbbing lip with ice cubes. The trouble with that was I'd never get all of it, especially right under my nose, and I ended up looking like a certain Nazi dictator. But now I'm older. I've matured. I've discovered hot wax. It still hurts, but as my mom always said, "You have to suffer for beauty."

Now I'm older, but unlike that old hair-color commercial, *You're not getting older, you're getting better,* I don't think I am getting better. I'm forty-four this year, and the truth is, I'm feeling a bit on the un-attractive side. Kinda old, kinda blah. My observant younger daughter (whom I am considering selling to the lowest bidder) recently pointed out that the lines around my mouth make me look like a ventriloquist's dummy. "But at least it draws attention away from your crooked nose!" she said. (Do I hear a bid for a buck-seventy-five?)

Then there's everything that's fallen. I'm considering buying myself a garter belt to wear around my neck just to keep my sagging body parts from dragging in the dust. It's not a pretty sight, to be sure. Sigh.

That's not to say I haven't had a few fleeting moments of beauty. As a part-time reporter for my local paper, I occasionally have to set up interviews with strangers, and I often suggest we meet someplace like

McDonald's. Invariably, the person will ask, "How will I recognize you?"

"Picture Cindy Crawford," I'll say. For that one moment, *I'm beautiful.*

What I really hate are photos of myself. I especially hate the ones in which I think I look exceptionally awful and someone comes along and says, "Oh, that looks just like you!"

I know I'm being hard on myself. I'm not that bad. On my desk there's a Peanuts comic strip with Peppermint Patty looking at herself in the mirror and telling her friend Marcy, "I don't look so bad after all! That's always been my ambition…to not look so bad after all." Not me, Patty—I want to be pretty. *Dear Lord, why can't I be pretty?* It's a prayer I've prayed off and on most of my life. *Make me pretty, Lord! (Pretty please?)*

Instead of being made pretty, God chose to make me beautiful.

Have you ever noticed how beautiful Christian women are? This puzzled me for the longest time. I'd sit in church and look at the women around me and be struck by their beauty, although on closer study I realized few of them had perfect figures or features. It's always been a real head scratcher. Recently, however, I discovered their secret. They're lifelong members of God's Beauty Spa—and so, it seems, am I.

In God's Beauty Spa, there are two treatments used in conjunction with each other. The first involves pain and suffering, much like plucking out unwanted facial hair but usually more painful, producing many more tears and sometimes lasting a lifetime. The apostle Paul described this treatment when he wrote, "We are hard pressed on every side, but not crushed; perplexed, but not in despair; persecuted, but not abandoned; struck down, but not destroyed…. Though outwardly we are wasting away, yet inwardly we are being renewed day by day. *For our light and momentary troubles are achieving for us an eternal glory that far outweighs them all*" (2 Corinthians 4:8-9,16-17; italics mine.) Treatment No. 1 is the purifying effect of all our sorrows—the financial calamities and wayward children, the cancer and alcoholism, divorce, depression, and just plain growing old. It's all the stuff we hate yet can't do a thing about. Treatment No. 1 strips us of our own beauty and readies us for Treatment No. 2.

Moses was the first person in the Bible to receive Treatment No. 2. When he came down from Mount Sinai with the stone tablets containing the Law, his face shone with radiance—a mere reflection of the Lord's glory. Now we, too, shine "with the brightness of his face. And so we are transfigured...our lives gradually becoming brighter and more beautiful as God enters our lives and we become like him" (2 Corinthians 3:18, MSG).

Treatment No. 2 is this: not our own beauty, but *God's* beauty. If he dwells in us by his Holy Spirit, then we reflect his glory, *his very nature.* And this is the beauty we reflect:

He is our Creator—we are his works of art. "For we are God's workmanship" (Ephesians 2:10).

He is our Shepherd—we who were lost now are found. "I am the good shepherd; I know my sheep and my sheep know me" (John 10:14).

He is our Maker and husband—we are wildly adored and no longer alone. "For your Maker is your husband" (Isaiah 54:5).

He is our mansion builder—we don't have to be consumed with building our own houses here on earth because this is not our real home. "In my Father's house are many mansions.... I go to prepare a place for you" (John 14:2, KJV).

He is our provider—we have enough for today. "So do not worry, saying, 'What shall we eat?' or 'What shall we drink?' or 'What shall we wear?' For the pagans run after all these things, and your heavenly Father knows that you need them. But seek first his kingdom and his righteousness, and all these things will be given to you as well" (Matthew 6:31-33).

He is our peace—we are no longer his enemy. "For he himself is our peace, who has made the two one and has destroyed the barrier, the dividing wall of hostility" (Ephesians 2:14).

He is almighty—we are safe. "He who dwells in the shelter of the Most High will rest in the shadow of the Almighty" (Psalm 91:1).

He is merciful—we are grateful. "He saved us, not because of righteous things we had done, but because of his mercy" (Titus 3:5).

There's *more:*

His purpose…gives us purpose. "The LORD will fulfill his purpose for me" (Psalm 138:8).

His promises…give us hope. "The LORD is faithful to all his promises and loving toward all he has made" (Psalm 145:13).

His presence…brings us constant companionship. "God is our refuge and our strength, an ever-present help in trouble" (Psalm 46:1).

His power…he gives to us. "I pray that out of his glorious riches he may strengthen you with power through his Spirit in your inner being" (Ephesians 3:16).

His faithfulness…gives us security. "Know therefore that the LORD your God is God; he is the faithful God, keeping his covenant of love to a thousand generations" (Deuteronomy 7:9).

His forgiveness…should cause us to shout, *Hallelujah!* "If we confess our sins, he is faithful and just and will forgive us our sins and purify us from all unrighteousness" (1 John 1:9).

His protection…keeps us from harm. "The angel of the LORD encamps around those who fear him" (Psalm 34:7).

His grace…enables us to bear pain. "My grace is sufficient for you" (2 Corinthians 12:9).

His strength…makes us strong. "Be strong in the Lord and in his mighty power" (Ephesians 6:10).

His discipline…makes us holy. "God disciplines us for our good, that we may share in his holiness" (Hebrews 12:10).

His Father-heart…makes us no longer orphans, but much-loved children. "But you received the Spirit of sonship. And by him we cry, 'Abba, Father'" (Romans 8:15).

His holiness…makes us awe-struck and inspires us to worship. "Holy, holy, holy is the LORD Almighty" (Isaiah 6:3).

He is just. He is good. He is all-powerful and patient. He is our help, our shield, our stronghold, our salvation. He is a mighty warrior who fights our battles for us. He is a benevolent King and a tender-hearted Shepherd.

He is the Living Word, the Sermon on the Mount, and the Fruit of the Spirit. He is 1 Corinthians 13, which says, *Love is patient, love is kind. It does not envy, it does not boast, it is not proud, rude, self-seeking, easily-angered; it doesn't keep a record of wrongs, it doesn't delight in evil, but rejoices with the truth; it always protects, always trusts, always hopes, always perseveres.*

This is the beauty we reflect, and all we need to do to obtain it is remain in relationship with the Lord. Does this mean if someone offered me free plastic surgery I wouldn't take it? Hmm… Even if I did, there'd be no guarantee I'd be any prettier, so I'd probably decline. Besides, *this* is the face God designed just for me. Quirky? Definitely. Pretty? I have my good days. Beautiful?

Yes.

Lord,

For whatever reason, you made blowfish and armadillos and ugly-looking reptiles—and you made me. Thank you that I am fearfully and wonderfully made, and because your Spirit lives in me, I am also beautiful. Amen.

THINK ON THESE THINGS

- If you could change anything about your appearance, what would it be? What differences would it make in your life? In your relationships? Now name your best feature(s). How else are you "fearfully and wonderfully made"?

- Proverbs 31:30 says, "Charm is deceptive, and beauty is fleeting; but a woman who fears the LORD is to be praised." To what extent have you pursued charm and beauty? How would you explain this verse to a friend who thinks she's unattractive?

- In thinking about how we as Christians reflect the Lord's glory, what attribute of God is most meaningful to you? Why? Choose an attribute that you would like to know more about and do a word study on it.

- "Would you see true beauty? Look at the pious man or woman in whom spirit dominates matter; watch him when he prays, when a ray of the divine beauty glows upon him when his prayer is ended; you will see the beauty of God shining in his face."— Girolamo Savonarola, *28th Sermon on Ezekiel*, c. 1489.

God Says, "Low, I Am with You Always!"

MAKE ME UNAFRAID

Fear makes the wolf bigger than he is.

UNKNOWN

Ever since I can remember, I've been afraid. More scared than a scaredy-cat. More cowardly than the lion in *The Wizard of Oz*. Able to sense man-eating bunny rabbits from a mile away. Look! Up in the sky! It's... *falling!*

I could blame this yellow stripe down my back on my parents. After all, statistics show that the most fearful people walking around are firstborn daughters. (That's me.) I could blame it on my dad, who once put a stocking over his face as a joke, causing me to wet my pants.

Or I could blame Sam Lang, who told me in second grade that the Russians were going to drop a poison-mushroom bomb on

California, where we lived, and poison all our drinking water.

I could even blame it on Steve Aston, who introduced me to the Hairy Eyeball, a marble stuck in the cement wall on Chase Street. We had to pass it on the way to school, and he was the one who told me if I crossed directly in front of it something terrible would happen to me. I accidentally did once. I'm still waiting for the something terrible to happen.

I have a teenage daughter that wants blue hair and a "tasteful" tattoo. *I'm afraid.*

I know we have snakes in our yard, but do they climb trees and swoop down on the heads of unsuspecting people walking by? *I'm afraid.*

What if I accidentally go out in public without a supply of breath mints? *I'm afraid.*

What if I accidentally put my foot in the toilet when I'm blow-drying my hair and electrocute myself? *I'm afraid.*

What if I get to a drawbridge and the red light is blinking and I forget what to do and instead of stopping I keep driving (like I did the time I drove to Daytona)—only the next time I don't make it across before the bridge opens? *I'm very afraid.*

And don't even mention flying on airplanes! Hurling through space in a flimsy tin can, miles above *terra firma?* It's unnatural. Besides, as my friend JoAnna likes to point out, God clearly promises, "*Low,* I am with you always."

Unfortunately, airplane travel is almost a necessity these days, but fortunately I have help in overcoming my fear of flying. Every time I have to get on an airplane, my wonderfully supportive husband brings me to the airport, kisses me good-bye, asks me if my life-insurance policy is up-to-date, then offers me these soothing words of comfort: "Don't worry. One way or another, your plane's going to come down."

That's when I kick him in the shins.

Once I'm on the plane, I'm usually fine, especially since I've devised elaborate mind games to keep myself from jumping out the emergency exit or asking the pilot to pull over and let me out. I tell myself, "Planes don't crash at 10 A.M." Or, "Planes don't crash if I'm asleep." Or, "Planes don't crash in San Jose."

Throughout the entire flight I study the flight attendants' faces for signs of fear—if they're afraid, then I know it's time to panic— and make sure they know ahead of time that I've requested a noneventful flight. At the first jolt of turbulence, I repeat, "Like bumps in the road, these are just bumps in the clouds."

I tell myself, "God hasn't given me a spirit of fear; but of power, and of love, and of a sound mind" (see 2 Timothy 1:7). I pray and ask him to take my fear away once and for all.

But I'm still afraid.

As I said before, I've been afraid for as long as I can remember. I don't know what triggered it or the reasons behind it; it has just always been. Growing up I was scared of dogs, the hall closet, garbage disposals, and earthquakes. I lived in California—not even the ground I stood on was secure. One of my biggest fears has always been having an earthquake hit when I'm in the shower. It's not so much the ceiling caving in on me that I fear as it is the idea of rescue workers finding me naked.

I thought that when I joined the air force and moved away from California, my fears would go away, but they didn't. At age nineteen I traded the shaking ground for B-52 bombers that would surely crash through my bedroom window. I added a few more phobias along the way. I thought if I walked outside, the power lines would snap and electrocute me. Or if the power lines didn't get me, Mafia men driving by would shoot me. Or if they didn't get me, I'd drive my car into a telephone pole or off a bridge into the water. Or if the B-52s didn't crash through my bedroom window and kill me while I slept, they'd fall from the sky on top of my head while I was out walking.

I wasn't safe outside. I wasn't safe in my house. I wasn't even safe inside my own thoughts. At that time in my life, I had come to the conclusion that life was basically meaningless. You just mark time until you die. Maybe you go to Disney World or get married or win an award, but for the most part you just get up in the morning, you do your regular stuff, then you go to sleep at night. After you do that enough times, you die.

That thought terrified me most of all.

There I was, a twenty-three-year-old wife, mother of a toddler, and maker of chili for the guys on my husband's softball team. I tried my hardest to look normal on the outside, to be normal, but on the inside I was afraid from the minute I opened my eyes in the morning until I went to sleep at night. If I went to sleep. Sometimes I'd lie awake, watching my bedroom window, waiting for incoming aircraft. Occasionally I'd try to pray, but the only prayer that I could think of at the time was, "Now I lay me down to sleep. I pray the Lord my soul to keep. If I should die before I wake…"

God. All I remembered of him from my childhood was that he sends plagues and floods and turns people into pillars of salt. All I remembered of the Bible was some scary place in the middle that talks of the end of the world. I was afraid to live but more afraid to die. And I had nowhere to go. Until I ended up in the ladies' room in the building where I worked.

Earlier I mentioned Rita and her New Testament and how I prayed a sinner's prayer, but I didn't tell you about how she first pierced me with her sword. That happened the Friday before. We had been talking about heaven, and I made the comment that I thought everybody went there (although I wasn't sure—it was mostly wishful thinking). That's when she pulled out her sword (the Word of God) and pierced me through my heart. She said, "That's not what the Bible says."

That's all she said—"That's not what the Bible says." But it was enough to make me double over in pain. That scary book that talked about the end of the world said I wasn't going to heaven. I went home that night, and after everyone was asleep, I got out the Bible my aunt had given me years before and turned to page one. (There was no way I was going to start with the scary stuff in the middle.)

I guess I'll make this long story short. The more I read, the more of the gospel I remembered from my childhood: God the Father sent his only Son to live a sinless life, take upon himself the sins of the world, and die in the place of sinners. I remembered the first time I heard that Jesus died for sinners. I thought, "How nice of him. I wonder who they were?" I imagined sinners were ancient Romans wearing togas and sandals. But that night in my living room, I knew they included a twenty-three-year-old woman wearing a nightgown and slippers.

I thought about that for the remainder of the weekend until I finally met up with Rita and her New Testament on Monday morning. That's the day I became one of God's children. That's the day the B-52s stopped aiming for my bedroom window, the Mafia men decided not to drive down my street and shoot me, and the power lines decided not to snap. And the God who so terrified me as a child whispered my name and told me I never had to be afraid ever again.

This would be an excellent place to say, "And from that moment on all my fears and phobias completely disappeared, and I've lived in total freedom ever since." The problem is, that's not true. At times I'm still afraid. Very afraid.

What gives?

I'm not an expert, but I think I'm still afraid because fear is ingrained in me; it's part of my thought process from way back. It's part of my sin nature. It's also a habit. I automatically think fearful thoughts. *But God hasn't given me a spirit of fear but of power, of love and of a sound mind.*

He says, "Fear not, for I have redeemed you" (Isaiah 43:1). "Do not be terrified.... Do not be afraid.... Do not be fainthearted" (Deuteronomy 1:29; 1:21; 20:3).

But I am.

I'm afraid for two reasons. First, I'm afraid in situations where I feel I have no control. Despite the fact that I've never taken a single flying lesson, I foolishly think that if I'm the one flying the plane, I know we'll land safely. But trust a trained pilot? Trust God whom I cannot see? I'd much rather trust myself. But that equals pride, and pride equals sin.

Second, I'm afraid when I forget how much I'm loved by Almighty God. That's when I need to remind myself:

- That nothing can separate me from his love. Neither life nor death, neither growling dogs nor airplane turbulence, not even my own imagination can separate me from the love of God.
- That he goes with me—when the plane goes up and when it comes down. "Even though I walk through the valley of the shadow of death, *I will fear no evil, for you are with me*" (Psalm 23:4, italics mine).
- That if the Bible says "Fear not," God has made a provision for me to do just that.

In his book *Lord of the Impossible,* Lloyd John Ogilvie says fear is only a hairbreadth away from faith. Sometimes, as from the door of an airplane, that hairbreadth looks vast and uncrossable, yet I've found if I do the thing I'm most afraid of, I'm not so afraid anymore. In fact, I'm more afraid of flying when I'm on the ground than when I'm up in the air.

I've asked God a thousand times to remove my fear. He's chosen to give me opportunities to trust him instead. That's not saying that bad things won't happen even if and when I do trust God, but in those instances he promises sufficient grace when I need it most.

So I get on those planes, buckle my seat belt, and take a deep breath. I tell myself, "For you did not receive a spirit that makes you a slave again to fear" (Romans 8:15). I give up control I never had in the first place and prepare myself to soar above the clouds. I look out the window as we take off and remember the psalmist's words, "For great is your love, higher than the heavens; your faithfulness reaches to the skies" (Psalm 108:4).

And before I know it, I'm flying.

❧

Lord,

I hate being afraid. I hate the way it feels and the things it keeps me from doing. Mostly I hate that it means I don't trust you and that I think I can take care of myself better than you can. Oh, such arrogance! Save me from myself, I pray. Amen.

THINK ON THESE THINGS

- List some of your fears. Which ones are imaginary or irrational, and which ones are legitimate? What are the probabilities of what you fear actually happening? Find several scriptures that deal with fear and memorize them. Repeat them to yourself whenever you start to fear.

- Christian author Gerald May wrote in *Simply Sane,* "Fear in its purest form is a lack of confidence in God." What would you do for God if you were unafraid? Ask him now to give you the boldness and the opportunity to do it.

- Meditate on Psalm 27. Why should we not be afraid? What actions does the psalmist take in this psalm? What does God do for him? What will God do for you?

• "Courage is not acting boldly without fear; it is, rather, acting in spite of fear. When Paul said that God hadn't given the Christian a spirit of fear, he didn't mean there is no more fear. He meant, rather, that the debilitating fear which often paralyzes the Christian is not sold in the store of God."—Steve Brown, *Living Free*

ELEVEN

God Uses Cracked Pots and Crackpots

MAKE ME USEFUL

My spelling is Wobbly. It's good spelling, but it Wobbles,

and the letters get in the wrong places.

WINNIE-THE-POOH

I think everybody should have a teenage daughter (especially mine). Just when I think I'm hot stuff and start believing my press releases and my (albeit limited) fan mail telling me how extremely talented and gifted I am, Laura brings me down to earth with the truth. Like the time I posted a letter on the refrigerator from a woman in Allentown, Pennsylvania, who wrote, "Dear Nancy Kennedy, I love you. I love your gift of humor. You've taken the message in your book and have painted it with your vibrant personality and made it real, wonderful, funny, true and unforgettable. I am so impressed."

Laura walked by, read it, and rolled her eyes. "Mom, they only write that stuff because they don't know you."

Which is true. Which is also why I want to set the record straight right now and tell you who I really am.

I'm average.

If I were a sofa, I would be plaid. I'm Melmac plastic plates in a Dresden china world. I'm white bread and vanilla pudding. Jell-O. Green Jell-O with sliced pears. As for my talents, I have a few. I have an uncanny knack for remembering commercial jingles, including the Choo-Choo Charlie one for Good and Plenty candy that ran on television back in the sixties. I can make my thighs jiggle without moving a muscle. I make a mean low-fat tamale.

Probably my best talent is making other moms look good in comparison to me. Several years ago I ran into a friend in Wal-Mart who was searching frantically for last-minute Easter basket goodies for her kids. Full of self-doubt and insecurity, she turned to my older daughter and said with a sigh, "I bet your mom makes you and your sister beautiful baskets."

As I cringed, Alison snorted and set my friend straight. "Are you kidding? Last year my mom gave us each a pack of gum and a five dollar bill!"

The woman's transformation was truly amazing as she hugged me and cried, "Gee, compared to you, I guess I'm not so bad!"

Of course she apologized profusely at her uncontrolled, gleeful outburst, but I didn't mind. That's what I do. Sing antique commercial jingles, make my thighs quiver, scatter cornmeal around my kitchen, and make other moms look good.

But other than those extraordinary talents, I'm basically average.

The problem with that is, I want to be *more*. I want to be someone God can use.

If you've read any of my other books, you'll know that I love Grand Schemes. *Quests*. Big Plans. When I get An Idea, I chase after it with Great Passion. I do everything in Capital Letters…including Falling Down.

I'll never forget the one and only Bible study I ever gave. It was back when I was a Mature Christian. I'd been a believer for a while. At least a month or two. I'd asked God to use me in my neighbors' lives, and then I set out to Be Used by Him.

I'd been a believer long enough and I'd watched enough Christian television in those two months to know what Useful Christians were like: confident, knowledgeable, passionate. And they had great hair. The hair wasn't a problem. The rest I figured I could fake (or at least trust the Spirit to help me wing it).

About a week before the Big Day, I carefully hand wrote personalized invitations to the women in my apartment complex (whom I neither knew well nor particularly liked), slipped the notes under each of their doors, and then ran away before my neighbors saw me.

The day before my Big Moment of Usefulness, I went to the American Bible Society and bought each woman a Bible (hoping to illustrate Christian generosity) and wrote out an inspiring prayer. I'd chosen to teach the gospel of John and that afternoon thumbed through it, jotting down notes peppered with spiritual-sounding words that I'd heard before but didn't understand, like *justification, sanctification,* and *transfiguration.*

Then I baked cookies. Homemade sugar cookies. Fish-shaped home-made sugar cookies with the ancient symbol IXOYE meticulously piped in brown icing. I wanted all my guests to know exactly the kind of Useful Christian I was. I planned to tell them, "Once I was lost, but now am found, was blind, but now I see." I couldn't wait to let them know that each one of them could be a Useful Christian *just like me.*

The morning of my Life-Changing Event, the sun shone brightly just for me. It was a Day Made in Heaven. Not too cold, not too warm. A perfect day to be Used by God. I stashed away all my non-Christian books and magazines, put praise music on the stereo, set out my fish cookies and waited for my Moment of Usefulness.

After the first hour went by (and nobody came), I told myself, "I must've put the wrong time on the invitation." After the second hour, I told myself, "Maybe I put the wrong date." After the third hour, I told myself, "They're all a bunch of pagan sinners anyway."

After the fourth hour (as I wrapped my fish cookies in plastic), God spoke.

Actually, it was more of a laugh. *Child, what are you doing?*

"Trying to be Useful, Lord."

Did you really think fish cookies would impress your neighbors into the Kingdom?

"No, I thought my inspiring teaching would do that. Too bad I didn't get the chance to find out."

No, it would've been too bad if you did. Do you know why nobody came to your Bible study?

"Because they'd rather stay home and watch game shows than learn your Word?"

No.

"White sale at JCPenney's?"

No, Child. I kept them away as an answer to your prayer.

"But I prayed to be made Useful, Lord!"

I know. Making you into a useful vessel is exactly what I'm doing, and sometimes that means suffering a little humiliation. Trust me, you'll thank me for it someday.

The problem is, what I think is useful and what God thinks is useful are two different ideas. I think usefulness is being Grand and Inspiring, but when I try to be that, all I end up with is a plateful of fish-shaped cookies that nobody comes to eat. I think I need to be Billy Graham. God wants me to be graham crackers and milk to a small child.

I've told this story in another book, but it's a good one, so I'll tell it again. A few years ago we had a big storm that caused extensive flooding in homes by the Crystal River, including the home of my friend Joe Koch. Wanting to be Used by God, I set out to help Joe. I had Grand Visions of ripping out drywall and putting up Sheetrock and comforting him with "psalms and spiritual songs," as the scripture says. Helping. Doing Something Important.

Unfortunately, by the time I got to his house that day, a crew had already been there and finished all the neat stuff I wanted to do. Desperate to help, I looked around Joe's house, but all I could find was a pile of wet postage stamps on the desk and Joe sitting nearby not saying much of anything. I stood by him, making feeble chitchat and peeling stamps apart. As I set them out to dry, I babbled on and on about how he could reuse them with a bit of glue…blah-blah-blah.

Joe continued not saying much and mostly just nodded. When I finished my stamp peeling I left, feeling like a failure. I'd wanted to be Useful, and all I ended up doing was playing around with wet postage stamps. How ordinary. How *average*.

Except it wasn't ordinary to Joe. I found out weeks later that he had told everyone how much I had helped him that day. He had been almost in despair, he said, but his turning point came when I stopped to talk to him and peel his wet stamps.

I'm convinced that when I get to heaven, God's not going to commend me on my fan mail, on how many books I sold, or how brilliantly I might have spoken to an auditorium full of women. He didn't make me Barbara Johnson or Max Lucado. It's okay with him that I'm a former goof-off California Valley Girl that skated through high school and didn't finish college. It's okay with him that I don't have organizational skills or business savvy. Sometimes I think all I'm good at is showing up on time.

But God uses me. He uses my prayers at Moms In Touch for my daughter and her friends at her school. He lets me open my house to an odd assortment of teenagers to feed them Pop Tarts and Otter Pops, let them use my computer for their schoolwork, and take them to church. He strips me of my Grand Ideas and lets me peel stamps. He reveals my lack of love for others and my abundant love of self and creates in me a usable heart of compassion and genuine mercy.

He takes all my past experiences (including my failures), present gifts (average as they may be), and especially my weaknesses, and uses them to touch others for the Kingdom. Ironically, he uses me most when I'm least aware of it. That way *he* gets the glory and not me.

He never promised that I'd ever be rich or famous or able to inspire the masses, but he did say if he began a good work in me, he'd carry it on to completion until the day of Christ Jesus (Philippians 1:6) and he'd give me lots of good works to perform (Ephesians 2:10). All I have to do is make myself available.

That much I know I can do.

Lord,

Sometimes I can't imagine how you can use a self-centered, unimpressive nobody like me, but you can — and you do. In fact, you've used a bunch of nobodies: a coward like Gideon, a stutterer like Moses, a prostitute like Rahab, a scrawny shepherd boy like David, a doubter like Thomas. An average woman like me. Use me, Lord, I pray. Amen.

THINK ON THESE THINGS

- Think of the people God has used in your life. In what ways did they show Christ's love to you?

- Choose a Bible character. What were his or her weaknesses? Strengths? How did God use him or her to further his purposes? How can God use you?

- Read Romans 12:1-8. What does it mean to "offer your bodies as living sacrifices"? As you study the rest of the passage, choose the portions that are most meaningful to you and recite them back to God as a prayer.

- "Service for the Kingdom does not consist of what you do or what you give; it depends on who you are. When you give God control, he will give you ways to serve. You will not need to drum up any areas to be of use to God. He will give you a zestful, fruitful life purely as his gift to you because you gave your life to him."—June Gunden, *Women's Devotional Bible*

Twelve

It's Not Easy Being Green

MAKE ME CONTENT

Envy is blind to its own gifts—all it sees is what it doesn't have.

TRUMAN BROOKS III

Memo to Kermit the Frog: I totally understand. It's *not* easy being green. Of course, in your song you're probably talking about the color of your skin while I'm talking about envy. As in looking at life through green goggles.

You see there's this *woman.* I like her a lot and everything, but she has this black dress. Sleeveless, plain, straight. A simple black dress. I could have that black dress. But she has tan arms to go with it. *Thin,* tan arms. And long legs. What really irks me is the fact that she used to be heavier, more like me, but now she's not. *Grrrrrrrrrr.* And she looks *good. Grrrrrrrrrr.*

Then there's her job. She actually gets paid to plan parties and dinners and events like international cuisine festivals for her boss. She doesn't have to do any of the work either. She has "people" for that. I don't have "people." I don't even have a black dress. *Grrrrrrrrrr.*

I went to one of her events a few months back. She had her "people" transform an empty warehouse into a scene from *Gone with the Wind*, with Scarlett O'Hara look-alikes carrying trays of mint juleps as a dozen Rhett Butlers tended to the barbecue.

And fiddle-dee-dee, if she didn't wear that black dress.

Not only that, she served the most decadent cheesecake I'd ever eaten. Gooey, creamy. I ate two pieces. Then I found out each forkful contained a week's worth of fat grams and a month's worth of calories—and she didn't even eat one bite. *Grrrrrrrrrr.* Double *grrrrrrrrrr.*

Amended note to Kermit the Frog: I take that back. It is easy being green. Too easy. So I pray, "Lord, help me not envy my friend." And she gets a promotion. And a company car. And another "people." I don't even have one "people."

So I keep praying. Harder. "Lord! Just give me thin, tan arms, and I won't envy anymore. Give me a black dress and a figure to wear it, and I'll be content. I don't even want 'people.' I just want to be equal to my friend. (Or better. Better is definitely better.)"

I try with all my might not to envy, but the harder I try, the more envy I feel. I envy people who can eat anything they want and not gain weight. I envy people who can think fast on their feet and always have a perfect comeback. I envy people who know how to dance and people who don't have to worry about every dollar they spend. I envy my single, childless friend's flat stomach and my sister's commitment to

Jazzercize. I envy every inch of Cindy Crawford's entire body. I envy people who don't envy.

I even try to spiritualize my envy. I tell myself (with the hope that God will overhear), "If I had _____ (fill in the blank), I could be a better Christian." If *my* books were on the bestseller list, I could reach more people for the Kingdom. If I had wads of money like another friend does, I'd give more to charity and stop worrying about my finances. If I had a body like Cindy Crawford's—well, I'm still working on that one.

But if God's overhearing, he's not answering my prayer. So I try harder and pray harder. "Help me not envy, Lord!" I console myself concerning my lack of a big, new house like the one my neighbor down the street owns by telling anyone who will listen, "At least I don't have to clean a monstrosity like that." Or I revel in hearing the news that she has termites. I feel smug, superior, if only for a moment. Then it's back to envying again.

I rationalize and tell myself, *Envy's not so bad. It's harmless. It doesn't hurt anybody.* But I'm lying. Envy poisons my thinking and my affections for the people God tells me to love. Whenever I see my friend in her black dress and start thinking that I should be the one looking that good, I don't want to be around her. I stay on the other side of the room, avoid her attempts at conversation, lie to her and tell her I really must be going. I growl under my breath, and before I know it, I start wishing evil on her. *Maybe she'll gain all that weight back. Maybe the cleaners will lose the dress. Maybe I'll lose even more weight than she has and get my own black dress and look even better than she does.*

Pretty soon envy so corrupts my thinking that I lose all sense of reason. Last year I heard of a vinegar diet. The claim was that if you'd drink a teaspoon of apple-cider vinegar every day, you'd lose a zillion pounds in a matter of weeks. Although I'm normally a semi-rational woman, I was in a hurry to show up my friend and reasoned that if one teaspoon of vinegar a day was good, a tablespoon was better—and a fourth of a cup would be even better. (Note: It's not.) After downing two ounces of straight vinegar, I spent the rest of the afternoon doubled over with a bellyache. I smelled like a pickle jar for three days after that. All I got from my envy was gherkin breath.

Envy left unchecked exposes my basest nature. I don't really want to tell you this, but I feel I must. It's about a dinner I attended a few years back. To set the stage, you have to understand that I'm the "funny one." That's *my* role. It's expected of me to be the cutup at the table, to keep the conversation rolling, to set the tone. As far as I'm concerned, you can also be funny but not at *my* table.

Well, it seemed whoever made the seating chart didn't know the rule and sat another funny lady at the table. A *funnier* lady. Immediately she had everyone clutching their sides in laughter. Except for me. I sat there stone-faced and stone-hearted, filled with envy and venom. I hated her hair; I hated her outfit; I hated her voice. I hated every word that came out of her mouth because they should've been my words. How dare she usurp my role! It was all so trivial and petty, but that's what envy does to a person.

I knew I had a choice to make. I could either acknowledge that the table was big enough for two funny people, or I could be an even bigger jerk. The jerk gene being dominant, every time she opened her mouth, I beat her to the punch line with a zinger of my own. I dredged up material I'd read or bits I'd written and kept the ladies at the table (including her) in stitches. It was as if she didn't even know I'd declared war.

Afterward, as everyone was saying good-bye, she graciously told me how much she enjoyed meeting me and that she hoped we could meet again. I suddenly knew what a snake felt like, having reached an all-time low. So I faked it. Offered her a firm handshake and a full-toothed smile. Returned her compliment. Then before she could see through me and know what I was really thinking, I slithered off.

It was a long ride home that night. Later when I climbed into bed, I turned to my husband and poured out my heart: all about my friend with the black dress and Cindy Crawford's great body and Winona Ryder's perfect nose and the funny lady that night who caught everyone's attention. (I omitted a few select details, of course.)

I must've chewed Barry's ear off for half an hour before he got a word in. But instead of offering me the "There, there, poor baby" that I was looking for, he ruthlessly (in my opinion) pointed out all the good things in my life. Then he added, "What more do you want?!"

To avoid answering him, I pretended I'd fallen asleep. Still, his question haunted me. What more do I want? The truth, plain and simple, is this: I want more. I want what others have, and I don't want them to have it. I want their prestige and position, I want their abilities and honor. I want their stuff.

Ouch! Seeing how ugly that looks on paper, I'm tempted to erase it. The trouble is, I can erase my words, but not my envy—and my envy is ugly. At its very core it doubts God's goodness. It gets in his face and says, "All that you have graciously provided me is not enough." It kicks and screams like a toddler throwing a tantrum, leading to "disorder and every evil practice" (James 3:16) and rotting my very bones (Proverbs 14:30).

So what do I do about this problem I have? Try harder to get rid of it? Resolve never to be envious again? That doesn't work. It doesn't work to say, "Thou shalt not." Even though the Bible tells me to rid myself of such things as pride, selfish ambition, discontent, envy, and strife, envy isn't an outward behavior that I can curb or control. It's an inward issue, a heart disease. But it's not a disease without a cure. I'm cured (although never completely this side of heaven) as I exchange my grumbling for gratitude, my self-pitying complaints for Spirit-inspired thanksgiving.

It's praying *not,* "Lord, help me not envy," but "Lord, make me content with what I have." It's reminding myself that God is who he says he is—sovereign and good. He is the very One whom the psalmist said does not withhold *any* good thing from those whose walk is blameless (Psalm 84:11). If that's true, then whatever my lot in life, I have all I need.

Knowing that, however, isn't enough. I need to take action. To pray for the object of my envy: *Thank you, Lord, for the gifts you have given that other woman. Bless her wit; give her lots of opportunities to share her stories with others.* When I'm praying for blessings on someone else's life, there's no room for whiny comparing or complaining or fretting over what I think I deserve. Besides, I have exactly what God wants me to have. No more. No less. What I have is enough. What I have is *best.*

To want otherwise would only be wanting less.

❧

Lord,

You have given me great gifts to enjoy and use for your kingdom, and I dishonor you and bring misery upon myself by envying another's gifts. I humbly ask for your forgiveness and bask in your mercy. I rejoice in what you have given me, for godliness with contentment is great gain. Amen.

THINK ON THESE THINGS

- Martin Luther said, "We pray for silver, but God often gives us gold instead." In light of this topic, what's "gold" in your life? Are you content with it, or is there someone's "silver" that you desire? How does that affect your relationship with that person? With God?

- Read the account of Rachel and Leah in Genesis 29 and 30. What was their core problem? If you could advise these women, what would you tell them? Find scriptures to support your answer.

- Psalm 103 tells what God does for us. Choose one or two ideas from the psalm that particularly strike you and write a prayer of thanksgiving. Hang it on your refrigerator or keep it in your Bible as a reminder of how God has blessed you.

• "No matter how much we get, it never seems to be enough. What so few realize is that the problem is not our lack of things, the problem is that our soul is empty and hungers for God."—Bill Hybels, *Character: Reclaiming Six Endangered Qualities*

THIRTEEN

All Puffed Up and Ready to Pop

MAKE ME HUMBLE

We are all worms. But I do believe that I am a glow-worm.
WINSTON CHURCHILL

To be honest with you, I don't have a problem with my ego, mainly because it's bigger than the state of Montana and hard to escape. Not that I haven't tried. For years I've been practicing a convincing "aw shucks" shrug whenever I receive a compliment, giving at least the appearance of an ego under control. Most of the time I can pull it off too—and sometimes I even believe it. Outwardly, I'm as humble as the late Mother Teresa. Inwardly, however, lurks a monster.

The problem is, I love *me*. I tend to agree with my mother and my Aunt Gladys (who think I'm the cleverest kid on the planet). Up until a few years ago, I didn't think anyone else knew about this love affair I've been carrying on with myself. I thought I had everything under control until I stumbled upon a conversation between my daughter and her friend.

The friend asked, "Now that your mom's a published author, is she famous?"

My daughter snorted, then scoffed, "She is in her own mind!"

At the time I shrugged it off as youthful ignorance or maybe as a tinge of jealousy. (After all, I had been on radio and television.) Still, her comment bothered me. I wanted to be humble. After all, Christ was humble, and I did want to be like him. *Besides,* I thought, *humility would definitely be an asset to my public image. And if my own daughter thinks I'm proud, maybe others do too.*

All too aware of the proverb, "Pride goes before destruction, a haughty spirit before a fall" (Proverbs 16:18), I begged God, *Please make me humble—but please, please, please don't let me fall!*

Actually, the thought thrilled me. True humility is so attractive in a Christian, and how I wanted people to be attracted to me. I couldn't wait to exude humility. Fortunately I didn't have to wait long at all. The next day I received a call from our church secretary asking if I would give a testimony at the 8:15 service the following Sunday morning.

"Be brief," she said. "Just a few words about what God's done in your life lately."

I knew this was my moment of testing: *Will I or won't I respond humbly? If I whisper a meek, "Me? You want little, ol' me to get up in front of all those people?" God will know it's all an act. What, then, is the humble thing to say?*

I answered with a simple "Sure, I'd be honored," then hung up the phone, relieved that I'd acted humbly. *Way to go!* I congratulated myself as I ran to my closet to choose the perfect outfit.

As I pulled out my brown, pinstriped suit, I glanced at my reflection in the mirror and began reliving one of my favorite daydreams. There I am, a keynote speaker at a national conference in some faraway city (all expenses paid, of course). I'm on stage in a packed auditorium with a microphone in my hand, and I'm simultaneously imparting wisdom and keeping the audience in stitches with my wit and winning way with words.

"That Nancy Kennedy," the audience members say as they nudge one another, "she's too much!"

"Too much" is right, nagged a voice inside my head. *Don't you think you're making too much out of this?* I mulled that thought over for a few seconds, then dismissed it as nonsense and returned to my daydream. I imagined being greeted by wild applause as I stepped up to the podium and tossed my head in that madcap way of mine, my face aglow as I spoke the Word of God. All I could think about was that glow some Christians seem to have. I wasn't sure how they got it, but I asked the Lord to give me that spiritual glow too.

I spent the following week in front of my mirror practicing it. As I did, I'd think humble thoughts like *I don't deserve all this attention,* and *I'm just one, lowly cog in God's machine, just a pinkie toe in the body of Christ. Please, applaud the Lord, not me.*

As for my outfit, I decided against the brown suit and opted instead for my turquoise jumper because of the way it made my green eyes sparkle. With the combination of sparkling green eyes and spiritual glow—well, need I say more? I was ready.

On Sunday morning I awoke before the alarm, eager to give myself plenty of time to prepare for the worship service. I poured myself an extra big cup of coffee, glowed at myself in the hallway mirror, then sat down to relax with the Sunday paper.

The rest of the morning went smoothly. I arrived at church with time to spare. I'd forgotten my Bible, but I looked great. As I pulled into my parking place I whispered a brief, "Bless me, Lord," and went in to get "miked."

The deacon in charge handed me a clip-on microphone and a battery pack to hook on my belt. "You're hooked up to the sound system upstairs," he explained. "Just turn the knob to the left when it's your turn to speak."

What could be easier? I thought as I checked my watch. *And time to spare for a touch-up in the ladies' room.*

What happened next I blame on the full-length mirror. I entered the ladies' room and, upon discovering it empty, considered my reflection. Instantly I was back at my daydream podium, surrounded by wild applause. I grabbed my hairbrush like a hand-held microphone and urged the audience, "Please, please…sit down. You're too kind." I continued humbly thanking them. Then I launched into my opening joke. "A rabbi, a minister, and a priest walk into a restaurant—"

Mid-sentence, I saw it out of the corner of my eye. The knob of my real microphone had somehow turned itself to the left. Which meant On. Which meant everyone in the building could hear me.

My face grew hot, and for a moment I thought I had died. But I wasn't that fortunate. Instead, as the sparkle left my eyes and the glow drained from my face, I resigned myself to living out my remaining years amid the tile and porcelain of the church bathroom.

My heart pounded as I heard the organist begin the prelude. The pastor gave the morning announcements, then the congregation sang its first hymn. Halfway into the second hymn, I had one of those epiphanies that can occur only while cowering in a bathroom. In preparing for the worship service I'd picked out the right outfit and had the glow down pat, but as far as my heart was concerned, with my delusions of grandeur and illusions of importance, I'd been a first-class jerk.

I started to moan softly as a wave of emotions (not to mention nausea) rushed through me. Embarrassment, humiliation, terror, anger at my sin. I wanted to run away, but the only door led into the sanctuary. No escape.

My only escape was confession.

I'd asked to be made humble, but I hadn't expected it to be quite so painful, quite so...*humbling.* The most painful part was my realization that God hadn't finished with me. He had only scratched the surface. With my Montana-sized ego, I would require an entire lifetime to get it under control. Fortunately God is more than willing to take the time and do whatever is necessary, including having me make a fool of myself in the ladies' room at my church.

I began to cry, and then the choir began to sing. *A broken spirit and a contrite heart you will not despise....* How like God to remind me in the midst of my foolishness that he loves to forgive. In the remaining moments before it would be my turn to speak, I confessed my pride and arrogance, accepted God's merciful forgiveness, wiped my face, and opened the ladies' room door to face certain public humiliation.

That's when I discovered that although the knob had been turned to the left, the cord had come unplugged from the battery pack. No one had heard me after all! *No one would ever know.*

For that brief moment I tasted what it means to be humble. Humility has nothing to do with me but everything to do with Christ. It's not me imitating Christ or effecting a posture of piety. It's not "humble is as humble does," but "humble is" as I recognize and remember that, first and foremost, I came to the cross with nothing. If I am in Christ, I am neither a worm nor an exalted member of the royal court, but a much-loved child. Everything I am, everything I have, everything I do is my Father's gift to me. True humility comes whenever I gratefully recognize the Lord's blessing to me—including his blessing of discipline. I am humbled by his mercy and his kindness to me, a wayward child who loves the limelight a little too much.

Of course that isn't to say there won't come a day when my arrogance won't be made public. I'm easily deluded by my self-importance, and one day I just may need a fiery blast of humiliation. But for that one moment in the ladies' room at church, God kept my delusions of grandeur our secret. That's why, when I heard the pastor call my name moments later, I could make my way up the center aisle of the sanctuary truly humble, my green eyes sparkling once again, my face genuinely aglow…and a piece of toilet paper trailing from my shoe.

❧

Lord,

You hate pride, but you love me. And because you love me, you're more than willing to answer my prayer to be made humble. Thank you for being gentle with me. I don't deserve it, but I am grateful for it. Continue your work in making me humble, that I may always be genuinely aglow with your Spirit. Amen.

Think on These Things

- What is the difference between enjoying the gifts and talents God has given you and being prideful of them? In what areas of your life are you most proud?

- Proverbs 16:18 says, "Pride goes before destruction, a haughty spirit before a fall." Was there ever a time when a haughty spirit caused you to fall? What lessons did you learn from it?

- Meditate on Galatians 6:14. What does it mean to boast in the cross?

- "Humility is nothing else but a right judgment of ourselves."—William Law, *Christian Perfection*

PART THREE

Give Me

Delight yourself in the LORD
and he will give you the desires of your heart.

PSALM 37:4

❧

FOURTEEN

The Richest Little Poor Girl in Town

GIVE ME DAILY BREAD

It's not hard to meet expenses—they're everywhere!

READ ON THE INTERNET

I'm waiting for my personal check for $1,000 from Bill Gates to arrive any day now. Normally I don't pay any attention to get-rich-quick schemes or chain letters that promise I'll get $500,000 in a matter of weeks *just like Betty Albert from Some City, Indiana,* if I would just send one dollar to the first name on the list. This isn't like that. *That's* just foolishness. *This* is directly from Bill Gates, or at least someone who has it on good authority from someone who knows someone at Microsoft that the e-mail letter I received is indeed from Mr. Gates.

It couldn't be easier, said the e-mail. All I needed to do was forward this message, directly from Bill, to as many of my friends as I can—without duplicating any names—and as soon as 1,000 people get the e-mail, each of us would receive $1,000 *and* a copy of Windows 98 for our computers. I'm certain by now 1,000 people must have received the e-mail, so it's probably only a matter of days until my check comes. I hope so anyway. I surely could use that money.

I'm also waiting for the Jeep Cherokee that I'm going to win in a raffle, although that won't come until the day after Thanksgiving (or maybe not until Monday, seeing it's a holiday weekend and all). That's okay. The main thing is, I'm going to get a free car for a dollar. The way I see it, someone's got to win it, so it might as well be me. Right? Besides, God knows my little red Tempo is begging to be put out to pasture.

Don't get me wrong. It's not that I'm not willing to work for my money or that I want to get rich. I simply want a new car and a free $1,000 from Bill Gates. I want enough money in my checkbook at all times so if I have a whim one morning to get my carpet professionally cleaned, I can just call the guy up and not have to budget for it for three months prior.

I want enough money so I can buy fresh fruit *and* fresh fish *and* laundry soap *and* a box of Pop Tarts *and* a magazine when I stop by the market to pick up just a loaf of bread. And I'd like to have money left over to rent a movie on the way home. I want enough money in my checkbook so if I ever find a pale pink blazer in a store window, I can rush right in and buy it, whether it's on sale or not. No more lay-away. No more weighing options. No more standing in the condiment aisle deciding whether to buy the ketchup or the mustard because I don't have enough money to buy both.

I want enough money in my bank account so I don't have to worry anymore. An automatic deposit of $100,000 every three years sounds about right. Then I wouldn't have to keep bothering God about dental bills and kids' field-trip expenses and costly sounding noises from a car that's noisy enough.

I want enough money so I don't have to trust God anymore.

There, I've said it. The honest truth. *I don't want to have to trust God anymore.* But trust seems to be the key word involved in the answers to all my prayers, especially in this "Give us this day our daily bread" thing. Not that I don't want to trust God for daily bread; I just want a three-month supply of it in the freezer. And maybe a side of beef and a few chickens. But Jesus told his disciples to pray, "Give us this day our daily bread." Give us *this* day whatever it is we need in order to accomplish what our Father who art in heaven would have us do.

I don't know about you, but I'm a natural-born worrier. I hate surprises (unless they're flowers from my sweetie), and I especially hate not knowing things in advance. For this reason, praying for daily bread doesn't sit well with me. That's why I'd rather pray for monthly advance supplies.

Lord, you are my shepherd, don't let me want.
Please fill my pantry with canned, pitted black olives and jars
     of pimentos,
And line my shelves with cases of tomato soup and boxes
     of instant rice.
Let my pitcher ever-flow with sweetened ice tea.

May goodness and mercy follow me all the days of my life,
So I'll never have to ask you for a loaf of pumpernickel ever again.
Amen.

Unfortunately my prayer goes unanswered. It's as if God thinks that if he gives me more than I need, I'll forget him. That I'll rely on myself and on my own hoarded supply of bread and not go to him with my needs. Or that I wouldn't share it with anyone. How could he think that about me?

This bothered me for the longest time until I finally decided I'd show God how wrong he was. A few years ago I started stockpiling my shelves with food, hiding it behind dishes and glassware that I never used. I made it a point to buy two of everything: one for the family to eat, one to save. Eventually all my shelves bulged. I had food stashed all over the house. In my spare time, I'd open the cupboards in the kitchen and out in the storage room and just admire all my loot.

But then something strange came over me. I couldn't bring myself to use any of my stash. Even though I might've had seven cans of cranberry sauce, if I wanted to serve some for dinner, I *couldn't* use a can off the shelf; I had to go to the store and buy another one. Or I'd lie and say we didn't have any. Isn't that insane?

After a few months I found myself in a quandary. I was making chili and needed chili powder. I had two tins of it in my spice rack, but I didn't want to use them, and I didn't have time to go buy another. So I debated: break into my hoard or go without. I decided I could use the chili powder I had on hand just this one time, and I would get another one first thing the next morning.

Reluctantly I opened the container and shook chili powder into my pan of browned hamburger. And then I watched clumps of chili powder get up and scurry around the pan. I don't know what kind of bugs they were, but they definitely didn't like their little feet prancing through hot chili.

Out went that can of chili powder (and that night's dinner). Then, just in case a wayward bug had decided to visit the other chili powder container, I took a peek.

Out went *that* can of chili powder. And the cinnamon. And the nutmeg. And five boxes of instant rice, a dozen boxes of macaroni, scores of boxes of cereal, stuffing mix, cake mixes, pretzels, corn meal, flour, sugar, even all my precious Pop Tarts. It was an Insect Epicurean Extravaganza. *Come on over to the Kennedy's! The missus won't know— she never opens anything!*

All my effort was tossed into the garbage can. We ended up eating a hodgepodge of creamed corn, canned peaches, tuna, and cranberry sauce for dinner that night. The entire family agreed it was a less than stellar moment. Plus, the next day I had to use up the surplus money I had hidden away as well and call in the exterminator.

Once the exterminator took my check, I had a conversation with the Lord.

"I had bugs, God!"

Do you know why?

"Because I didn't put everything in glass jars?"

No, but I'll give you a hint. Do you remember what happened when I gave the children of Israel manna from heaven and they hoarded it until morning?

"Ugh—it stunk and was full of maggots!"

Do you remember why?

"Because they disobeyed. But I didn't! I just wanted—"

You just wanted to live your life apart from me. But I love you too much to let you do that. I want you to ask for what you need every day. I love to give good gifts to my children. However, sometimes my gifts are only enough for the day.

"But some of your other children have full pantries."

That doesn't mean I love you any less. Just remember I'll never give you a stone when you ask me for bread, nor a snake when you ask for a fish. But I want you to ask for what you need. That gives me a chance to show you my Father-heart toward you. It gives me pleasure to provide.

As a parent I can understand that. As a child I take delight when I receive a blessing from the One who loves me most. And because he loves me most, sometimes he strips away everything that is not bread in my life in order that I might recognize his bounty.

"Actually, I don't have a sense of needing anything personally," wrote Paul to the Philippians. "I've learned by now to be quite content whatever my circumstances. I'm just as happy with little as with much, with much as with little. I've found the recipe for being happy whether full or hungry, hands full or hands empty. Whatever I have, wherever I am, I can make it through anything in the One who makes me who I am" (Philippians 4:11-13, MSG).

Sometimes I have a lot. Right now for instance. As I write this, I have a few extra dollars in the bank (although the furnace has been making a clicking noise...). Other times I have to dig through the couch cushions in search of change. I've come to the conclusion that either way is fine with me. As odd as it sounds, the couch-digging times are even kind of fun. Those are the times I discover exactly how little I can do without and still sing for joy.

As for my personal check for $1,000 from Bill Gates, I won't turn it down if it comes, but if it doesn't, oh well. I have bread for the day. Really, what more do I need? I have a Father who loves me, and if for no other reason, that makes me the richest little poor girl in town.

✤

Father,

I worry and fret and search my checkbook and cry, yet you feed the sparrows and clothe the lilies of the fields. How much more you feed and clothe me! I know King David was telling the truth when he said he had never seen the righteous forsaken or your seed begging for bread. Thank you, Lord, for your abundant provision, and forgive me for ever doubting it. Amen.

THINK ON THESE THINGS

- "Bread" is more than just food; it's everything necessary for our physical, emotional, and spiritual well-being. How has God provided bread for you lately?

- A prerequisite to receiving bread is asking. What are some reasons people don't ask? Read Luke 11:1-13. What does this passage tell you about asking? If you have had trouble asking God for things, take this time to confess your reluctance. Now go ahead—ask!

- When it comes to daily bread, do you ever worry about having enough? In Luke 12:22-34 what did Jesus tell his disciples? Why should we not worry? Write your answer as a prayer of praise and thanksgiving to the Lord.

- "For when you mention and pray for daily bread, you pray for everything that is necessary in order to have and enjoy daily bread and, on the other hand, against everything which interferes with it."—Martin Luther

FIFTEEN

Patience Is Just Another Word for ARGGHHHHHH!

GIVE ME PATIENCE

It's easy to identify people who can't count to ten.
They're in front of you in the supermarket express lane.

BUMPER STICKER

The late Erma Bombeck claimed she lost it in the postnatal depression. As for me, I lost it in the Toys R Us parking lot in Salinas, California. Although it was nearly fourteen years ago, my kids still remember it as The Day Mom Went Cuckoo.

I already told you about the time I prayed for patience, back when Alison was a toddler, and how almost immediately she came down with chickenpox, ate the knobs off the stereo, smeared Vaseline on the mirror, and shoved a grape up her nose. So when Laura came along and unleashed previously unknown methods of driving a parent crazy (such as licking every surface she ever came in contact with), I cried out to God once more for a "supernatural sensation of well-being, equanimity, and composure." I was careful not to call it "patience," for I'd learned what would happen then. Besides, I had enough patience to last me a lifetime. I had patience up to my eyeballs. By the time Laura was two and Alison was eight, I was so patient it oozed out my pores. In fact, I was tired of being patient, and it was making me downright cranky.

So I loaded up the girls and drove to Toys R Us.

Looking back, the idea was doomed from the start. That morning my daughters had tortured and tormented each other until I cried. Laura had licked every door in the house and unwrapped (and licked) every bar of soap, while Alison begged for a dog. Nonstop. Then they both spilled the contents of the refrigerator onto the carpet one plateful, bowlful, and cupful at a time. That's when I decided a trip to Toys R Us might be a pleasant excursion for the three of us.

Oh, to be so naive again. Alison continued her campaign for a dog the entire eight-mile trip to Salinas while Laura rhythmically kicked me in the back from her car seat. Meanwhile a tape of Raffi played on and on and on and on and...

And Alison asked why couldn't we get a dog. And Laura kicked me. And Raffi sang about "Baby Beluga." And Alison asked...Laura kicked...Raffi sang...

AndAlisonaskedandLaurakickedandRaffisang...

By the time I hit the Toys R Us parking lot every iota of patience I had within me exploded out the top of my head. As the girls recall it, my head spun around, my eyes popped out, my hair stood on end, and steam shot out of my ears. I slammed on my brakes, threw the car into park, and ran out of the car making animal sounds and scream-ing. I yelled. I cursed. I yelled some more.

When I eventually got back into the car, both girls sat absolutely still for the entire ride home, not mentioning once that we never even made it into the toy store. Later that evening when Barry came home, the girls rushed up to him and clung to his legs and wouldn't let go. "Mommy went cuckoo," Laura told him. Alison ratted on me and told him I'd used a bad word. It was not my finest hour.

Ah, but that was eons ago. Today I look back on it and laugh. Today I am, as they say, cool as a cucumber. Sometimes I'm an entire salad, I'm so cool. In fact, I was thinking about it just the other day, about how far I'd come, how my life could easily be a walking billboard for Patience. Maybe I should teach a class on it at church. So many of my friends struggle with impatience—and, well, at the risk of sounding arrogant, I don't.

Anyway, I was driving along, thinking about the whole subject of patience when a feeling of calmness and tranquillity came over me— the feeling I had prayed for years earlier. *Finally,* I thought. *God has finally answered one of my prayers exactly the way I had hoped he would.*

Do you know what "earthquake weather" is? It's not an official meteorological term, but we native Californians know that just before an earthquake hits, the air gets eerily still and oddly warm and the birds disappear. Here in Florida a similar thing happens before a tornado. Calmness and tranquillity.

So I was driving along, enjoying the delicious fruit of patience, won-dering what I could pray for next. (Kindness? *Maybe.* Gentleness? *I'm already fairly gentle.* Self-control? *Not when there's a bag of miniature*

Snickers bars at home waiting for me to eat them.) As I weighed the possibilities, all of a sudden I realized the car behind me was practically in my trunk and *wouldn't* back off.

Ever patient, ever calm, I sped up a bit, then pumped my brakes, then sped up, then braked. I kept at it the entire three-and-a-half miles down the street to the signal. *Cool as a cucumber,* I reminded myself. *Remember, you're the patient one here.*

I sat at the red light in the right-hand lane, still patient, still cucumber-cool. All was well with my soul…until the tailgating driver decided that she wanted to turn right and honked at me to go. Well, I didn't want to turn right. (Actually I did, but since the other driver was being such a jerk, I changed my mind.) So I sat there. Patiently. In fact, I was so patient, I nearly forgot to go once the light turned green. I may have even sat there for thirty seconds or so.

Next I calmly drove to the bank, patiently circled the parking lot with my fingers clenched around the steering wheel, parked, walked inside, stood in line, and tapped my feet. Then I moved to a shorter line. Then to an even shorter line. Then behind a shaky elderly woman who took *forever* doing whatever she had to do, which in my opinion could've waited until later that afternoon.

After the bank I went to the market, where someone's wobbly wheeled, screeching cart serenaded me throughout the entire store. By the time I made it to the checkout line, I understood the phrase "torques my jaw." I'd clenched my teeth so tightly against the grating noise I thought my jaw would break. And then I discovered I was in line behind that same elderly woman from the bank, and she clearly couldn't read the "10 Items or Less" sign because she had *fifteen* items. *And* she paid by check. *And* she couldn't find her pen. But I kept my cool, only rolling my eyes at the clerk once when the lady wasn't looking.

Next I went to the copy place, where some woman took her sweet time copying Yahtzee score papers, tying up the machine while she tried to figure out how to make two-sided copies. *Who cares about Yahtzee?* I thought as I waited with my stack of papers. *My stuff involves ministry.* After taking *forever,* she argued with the clerk about whether she had to pay for "mistakes." It was a good thing I'm a patient person because I was about to tell her—well, never mind.

By the time I got home, I discovered I'd missed the beginning of a TV show I'd wanted to watch. Then a Special Bulletin interrupted it. When the show resumed, the audience was laughing, and I had missed what was so funny. Then the phone rang, interrupting the show *again*—and it was a wrong number. Then it rang again. Then the phone rang *again*—once. By the end of the afternoon, my cucumber-like coolness had begun to wilt. I mustered up all the patience I could, not wanting to ruin my cool reputation.

Then the earthquake hit.

The phone rang again. This time it was a telemarketer asking me about termite inspection. Or was it burial plots? I couldn't hear him over the rumbling—*my rumbling.* All of a sudden, I exploded. It was Toys R Us all over again. "I've had it!" I screamed into the phone. "I don't know what you're selling, nor do I care. I'm in the middle of something *important!*" I continued ranting about anything and everything, about slow elderly women and tailgaters, voice-mail mazes that never allow you to talk to a real human, husbands who leave their work boots in the middle of the floor, kids who leave packages of lunchmeat open, busy signals and answering machines—and people who *don't* have them.

I started to say, "And telemarketers like you really grate on my nerves," but he hung up on me. I don't know what came over me, but the next thing I knew, I yanked the phone off the wall. Just as I was about to toss it through my front window, I had a vision. I saw myself fourteen years earlier, howling like an animal in a toy-store parking lot. Nothing had changed. Except now I had a few gray hairs.

The revelation both shocked and horrified me. I thought I had come so far, yet I hadn't progressed an inch. I vowed to try harder, to think patient thoughts and be a better person, even though I knew all that was futile. I remembered something Paul wrote in Romans: "For I have the desire to do what is good, but I cannot carry it out. For what I do is not the good I want to do; no, the evil I do not want to do— this I keep on doing" (7:18-19). Me, too. The harder I try, the more miserably I fail.

On the other hand, when I put the last fourteen years under a microscope, I find I *have* made progress. Patience is a fruit of God's Spirit, and because we who are in Christ are "controlled not by the sinful nature but by the Spirit," (Romans 8:9), God will produce his fruit in me as long as I remember to sow to please him (Galatians 6:7-8). Times like these are just setbacks to remind me once again that I am and always will be until I die, a sinner in need of grace.

This was also God's continuing answer to my prayer. I prayed for patience; he sent irritations and petty annoyances. "Be happy," says the apostle James, "for when the way is rough, your patience has a chance to grow" (James 1:2-3, TLB). I may never jump for joy over kids who lick things and telemarketers who call to sell me things I don't want, but I can rejoice because of the fruit they eventually help produce.

Next time I hope I'll remember that *before* I tear the phone off the wall.

⳾

Lord,

Next time I'm tempted to erupt, please remind me not to. Remind me instead of your grace to endure and of the pearl you're fashioning from these very irritations. Let me take a lesson from the oyster and let you do what needs to be done—patiently. Amen.

THINK ON THESE THINGS

- In what area of your life are you most impatient? What usually happens when you are impatient?

- What does patience look like? How would your life be different if you responded to irritations with patience? Read James 1:2-3 in a variety of Bible translations. Ask God to help you consider your trials "pure joy."

- Galatians 5:22 lists the fruit of the Spirit (which includes patience). What is needed for fruit to grow? Colossians 3:12 says, "Therefore, as God's chosen people, holy and dearly loved, clothe yourselves with compassion, kindness, humility, gentleness and patience." How are we to "clothe" ourselves with these virtues? See Colossians 1:11-14.

• "God grows patience in our lives as we see his great patience with us. When we picture how long-suffering and patient God has been with us it seems to just melt away our impatience. God slowly softens our hard hearts and quietly replaces them with an attitude of tolerance, understanding and forbearance."—Bill Hybels, *Character: Reclaiming Six Endangered Qualities*

Sixteen

If You Hear the Toilet Flush and the Word "Uh-oh," It's Already Too Late

GIVE ME WISDOM

You're never too old to learn something stupid.

ANONYMOUS

I know stuff. I don't know how I know it, I just do. Like, only 30 percent of people can flare their nostrils. A *jiffy* is 1/100th of a second, and 33 percent of women lie about their weight. (I weigh 123 pounds.)

I know that the Spanish moss that hangs from my oak trees is a parasite from the pineapple family and that BTU's are British Thermal Units (which, if I leave the front door open when the air conditioner is on, are wasted and I get yelled at). I know that *dreamt* is the only English word that ends in "mt" and that "Kennedy" means "hideous head" in Irish.

As I said, I know lots of stuff, but knowing stuff isn't the same as having wisdom. I know that *now*, but I didn't know it *then*.

Then I grew up smart but not necessarily wise. As a child I knew that you could set a pile of leaves on fire by aiming a magnifying glass at it while outside, but I wouldn't have thought not to do it in the wind. In fifth grade, as a science experiment, I filled ten half-gallon jars with varying levels of water, plants, and snails. I don't remember what hypothesis I was trying to prove, but what I learned was this: If you leave ten jars of snails in water inside a classroom over Christmas vacation, all the snails will die and create a stench so putrid that rotten eggs smell like lilacs in comparison. Not only that, your gagging teacher will make you dispose of it all by yourself, no matter how much it makes *you* gag.

They say wisdom comes with age, but there's usually an exception to every rule. In an earlier book I wrote about the time I was sixteen and dumped a pot of hot red wax down the kitchen sink and chased it with cold water. I ended up with a candle shaped like a drainpipe, a plumber's bill for more than the national debt, and parents who considered having their daughter's name changed to Dennis (as in "the Menace").

Then there was the weekend after I got my driver's license. As my mom and dad left for a few days (big mistake), the last thing they said to me on their way out was, "no driving."

So as soon as they'd been gone a safe amount of time, I piled my sister and her friends into my mom's Ford LTD and headed for Featherly Park. Now, Featherly Park was about ten miles away, just off the freeway. Being an inexperienced driver, I did have enough wisdom not to use the busy freeway, choosing the road parallel to it instead. However, that's all the wisdom I had.

Although I used the road next to the freeway, I followed the freeway signs, including the one that said FEATHERLY PARK STAY LEFT. So I did. I got into the "left" lane (in reality, the oncoming lane of the two-lane road) and drove that way for miles. People from the freeway honked and shouted and waved at us, which I thought was sweet of them. I waved back. After all, I had my mom's car, and we were headed for Featherly Park.

It's only because God has mercy on idiots that I didn't cause any head-on collisions. By the time I reached the end of the road and realized the enormity of my stupidity and what might've happened, I outwardly shrugged it off in front of my passengers. But to this day I've never forgotten how dangerous a fool left to herself can be. "Experience comes from what we have done," someone once said, "but *wisdom* comes from what we have done badly." If that's true, then I qualify as the wisest woman on earth.

Recently I polled some friends about any words of wisdom they had. Here's what they said:

- If you're new at cooking, following a recipe is the safest course, no matter what the imagination says, especially when making a sauce. It's vitally important to use the correct proportion of thickener to liquid or—hello!—you end up with either a gumball or a watery mess and, either way, an unhappy family. Also, spices are good, but too much of a good thing equals a "throw-out."
- Never stop to tie your shoelace while in a revolving door.

- Check for toilet paper *before* you sit down.
- When your "check engine" light goes on, putting a piece of duct tape over it makes the light go away but not the problem.
- Never smack a man chewing tobacco.
- Don't sneeze when you're getting your hair cut.
- Rules are boundaries that keep us from going overboard.

I don't know about you, but I need these bits of wisdom that have been born of experience. Also, I'd much rather learn from others' mistakes than from my own. Some say that's true wisdom, but there's a wisdom even greater than that, and that's the wisdom for which I pray.

Frankly, I'm an idiot. Most days I don't know the first thing about being a wife or mother—or even a human being. If it weren't for God's wisdom, I'd botch up everything. The Lord knows that, too, which is why, when I pray for wisdom, he gives it generously without calling me a dimwit (James 1:5, my paraphrase).

I come to God with my questions, both significant and trivial. Should I confront a Christian friend who's dating an unbeliever? Should I take this job I've been offered? When is my daughter old enough to shave her legs? How do I know when/if she's ready to drive or date? When should I call the doctor? How can I tell if this "new" teaching I'm hearing about is really just an old lie of the devil?

Whether from a specific scripture, a general Bible principle, or a word from a trusted and tested elder or counselor, God's wisdom is sweet to my soul. As Proverbs 24:14 tells me, when I find it, I find a hope that can't be cut off. The Bible also says God's wisdom is a shelter, preserving the life of its possessor (Ecclesiastes 7:12) and brightening a man's face (Ecclesiastes 8:1). It's more precious than rubies (Proverbs 8:11), better to obtain than gold (Proverbs 16:16), and will save me from the ways of wicked men (Proverbs 2:12).

"The fear of the LORD is the beginning of wisdom," say both King Solomon, the wisest man who ever lived, and Alpha, a seventy-something widow from Texas who has walked with Jesus for the last sixty-four years. She says, "I used to have a lot of 'If onlys' in my vocabulary, but now I'm thankful for hard times because God knows I need them. I just trust that he knows best because he *is* wisdom."

"Trust in the LORD with all your heart and lean not on your own understanding," my ninety-six-year-old friend Geneva White used to advise me. "In *all* your ways acknowledge him, and he will make your paths straight" (Proverbs 3:5-6, italics mine). Geneva should know; he made her path straight for over eighty years. In her last days, she would say her eyes were dim and her "mind's like a sieve these days," but she was wise enough to know not to trust in herself. That's what fools do, according to King Solomon (Proverbs 28:26).

Betty, a follower of Christ from the time she was an eighteen-year-old World War II bride, offers this wisdom: "To me, knowing and walking with the Lord and staying in his Word is wisdom. Psalm 119:99 says, 'I have more insight than all my teachers, for Thy testimonies are my meditation' (NASB). No matter what the world calls wisdom, the *truth* is in God's Word."

Sometimes I listen to these women and wonder if I'll ever be wise, especially when I consider all the foolish things I still do every day. I know a lot of stuff, but too often I lack common sense. However, the good news is that even a fool like me can become wise if she seeks her wisdom from God through his Word.

The best news is that it's not hard to find. In Paul's prayer for the church at Colosse, he asked that they might "have the full riches of complete understanding, in order that they may know the mystery of God, namely, Christ, *in whom are hidden all the treasures of wisdom and knowledge*" (Colossians 2:2-3, italics mine). In the margin of my Bible I've written, "God doesn't hide his wisdom *from* us, but *in* us, if we are in Christ and we hide his word in our heart."

"The law of the LORD is perfect, reviving the soul," wrote King David in Psalm 19. "The statutes of the LORD are trustworthy, making wise the simple. The precepts of the LORD are right, giving joy to the heart. The commands of the LORD are radiant, giving light to the eyes" (vv. 7-8). Most important, "the fear of the LORD," which is where wisdom begins, "is pure, enduring forever" (v. 9). All who find it will never be put to shame.

I know that.

⌘

Lord,

A wise woman builds her house, but with her own hands a foolish woman tears hers down. Without wisdom I am as dangerous as a hurricane. May I value wisdom above all else. Thank you, that you give it generously to those who ask. Amen.

THINK ON THESE THINGS

- What wisdom have you gathered over the years? What do you think is the difference between knowledge and wisdom? What is the importance of each?

- Go through the book of Proverbs and list wise statements that apply to your life right now. If you were to follow them, how might your situation be different? Memorize the most relevant proverb(s) to help you make wise decisions.

- Read 1 Corinthians 2. Contrast the wisdom of this age with the wisdom of God. What kind of foolishness is going around your community? How would you confront it? Here's a challenge: Research the latest "new" teaching and have on hand the scriptures that refute it (making sure you keep them in context). Ask God for the wisdom to discern truth from error, then trust that he will. Bonus question: What does it mean, "We have the mind of Christ" (v. 16)?

- "Wisdom is the power to see and the inclination to choose the best and highest goal, together with the surest means of attaining it."—J. I. Packer, *Knowing God*

SEVENTEEN

"Drive," He Said

GIVE ME A PURPOSE

A dairymaid can milk cows for the glory of God.

MARTIN LUTHER

I think it was Lily Tomlin who said, "I always wanted to be somebody, but I should have been more specific." Well I, too, always wanted to be somebody, and I *was* specific. From the time I was old enough to say "egocentric narcissist," I've wanted to be Somebody Important. To win an Oscar or an Emmy, a Pulitzer, or at least the Publishers Clearinghouse Sweepstakes. I've had an acceptance speech ready for any kind of award that might come my way:

I am both humbled and honored to receive this award. I want to thank the Academy; and my mom and dad for putting up with me; my kinder-garten teacher, Mrs. Adamson, for letting me be Blackboard Monitor; and my eighth-grade drama teacher, Mrs. Melke, for choosing me for the lead in Our Town *(and for not flunking me when I went on stage chewing gum and nearly choked while delivering my lines). I also want to thank God for making who and what I am today.*

I've always wanted to be somebody who inspired the masses and captured the hearts of the multitude. To have the compassion of Mother Teresa, the influence and genuine appeal of Oprah Winfrey, the warmth of Barbara Bush, and the wardrobe of Princess Diana. I wanted my life to have Purpose and Meaning and plenty of brown-sugar-and-cinnamon Pop Tarts. So I prayed, "Lord, give me a grand purpose in my life." Then I sat back and waited for him to call me into the limelight. Instead God handed me two daughters and a set of car keys. "Drive," he said.

It took me more than twenty years, but I've finally come to the conclusion that my purpose in life is to drive girls. To the mall and to volleyball practice. To softball games and to the mall. To the mall and youth events. To the beach. To school. To the mall. To the mall in the next town. To Taco Bell.

Basically it's simple. From the beginning, I had a car, they didn't. They needed a ride. I had a choice: Drive them and their myriad close, personal friends wherever they want to go, or let them get into cars driven by somebody's sister's boyfriend's friend appropriately named "Crash."

Of course it didn't start out that way. It started out with just the two of them arguing over who got dibs on the front seat or fighting over breathing each other's air in the backseat. Then I got smart and added a friend or two. I reasoned that if they each had someone else to divert their attention away from pestering each other, they wouldn't pester me. (Heh heh heh. I'm not as dumb as I look.) So from the time I could round up some extras, wherever we went, instead of two girls I had at least three or four. The other moms in the neighborhood dubbed me Transportation Central. Some even hailed me as Taxi Queen.

Back when the girls were younger, my role consisted mainly of making sure everyone had her seat belt buckled and grabbed the right backpack once she got home. I controlled the radio and tape player. I determined the route. The rules were simple: All body parts must remain inside the car at all times, and everyone needs to "go" before we leave.

Now that they're older, my role hasn't changed, although the rules have gotten a bit more rigid—their rules, not mine. Mine are basically the same, except I've added: *No challenging cute guys in monster trucks to a drag race when I'm stopped at a red light,* and *If you must shriek every time you talk about Leonardo DiCaprio, warn me in advance so I can plug my ears.*

As for their rules, the condensed version boils down to one word: don't. Don't wear *that* (which covers just about every outfit I own). Don't have a "Honk if you love easy listening" bumper sticker on your car. Don't honk at anyone else's bumper sticker. *Don't honk.* Don't wave to anyone. Don't sing with the radio. Don't drive past anyone we might know. If at all possible, be invisible (especially if you're wearing *that*).

Most important, I can't let anyone they might know see them being dropped off or picked up. My husband doesn't understand this. He believes if a person is going to the movie theater on Main Street, the logical place to be dropped off is in front of the theater on Main Street. (That's why I'm the driver. I understand these things.)

"Poor baby," I told my bewildered other half the day our older daughter came storming into the house muttering something about "ultimate humiliation" and "total degradation" after he met her and her friends *at the theater entrance.* "Obviously you've never been a fourteen-year-old girl."

I, on the other hand, have been. That's why I drive.

Actually, driving girls has proven to be educational. For example, I know every drive-through burger place and every gas station where Major Babes work, as well as every street that every past, present, and future boyfriend lives on. I've driven to every mall in central Florida, every high-school stadium in our division, and every office-supply store in North America that sells folders with pockets *and* prongs. I know who's dating whom and who's about to break up. I even know the entire plot line of every episode of *Party of Five.*

My car's been used as a cafeteria, a beauty parlor, and a dressing room. A last-minute study hall and a place to take a nap.

A confessional and a sanctuary.

Something happens within my little red Tempo when it's filled with girls.

God enters.

He's not always evident to the gigglers in the backseat, and often he can't be heard over their chatter mixed with Pearl Jam, but he's there just the same. I know it, and every once in a while the girls know it too.

"Mrs. Kennedy, why do you have an 'Enjoying God' bumper sticker on your car?" "How do you know which church teaches the right thing?" "Why do you think Ouija boards are so bad?"

We've discussed Buddhism and paganism, sex, lies, and Marilyn Manson. Sometimes I'm able to pray out loud for them. (I *always* pray silently.) Occasionally they even acknowledge my humanity and ask about my life. Mostly, though, I just drive.

As much as I love this chosen calling, it does have its drawbacks, such as the 140,000 miles on my eight-year-old car—139,000 of which were used driving girls no farther than fifty miles from home. Not to mention an interior permeated with the odor of acne cream and Calvin Klein *Obsession,* the footprints on the ceiling, and the lip prints I found on the back window last week. (I don't even want to know.)

It's not always convenient either, especially when I'm snug at home, falling asleep in front of the TV at 9:30, and I have to pick the girls up from the football game at ten. Or when Girl #1 lives ten miles in the opposite direction from Girl #2, or when someone forgets her jacket and will get *killed* if she comes home one more time without it. ("Please, Mrs. Kennedy, have pity on me just this once!")

I confess, I'm not always the merriest mom behind the wheel, especially when I let my mind wander to what my life might've been. I wanted fame and recognition. I got obscurity and a backseat full of Skittles wrappers. I wanted to inspire the masses. Instead I meekly follow strict instructions *not* to drive past the group of boys standing by the football field on my way out of the high-school parking lot in the mornings.

I wanted to be Somebody Important. I ended up driving girls. It's not what I envisioned for my life, but it's what I was created to do. And over the years I've come to embrace it—and love it. "'For I know the plans I have for you,' declares the LORD, 'plans to prosper you and not to harm you, plans to give you hope and a future'" (Jeremiah 29:11). He has done just that.

A few months ago a friend asked me what I wanted on my tombstone. At the time I said something like "She forgot to duck." But after having had time to mull it over, I can think of no greater epitaph than "She drove girls." It doesn't matter that no one will understand. God will, and I hope the girls I've driven will. And maybe because of the time spent inside the sanctuary of my car, despite its noisy muffler and the odd cracking sound it makes when it's hot outside, maybe my passengers over the past twenty years will have been eternally changed. I know I've been.

I don't know why God does what he does, but I do know that he has called me to this, at *this* time in history, in the lives of *these* girls, for his purpose. It's not lofty, but it's heavenly. It'll never win me a Pulitzer, but it will earn me a crown.

❧

Father,

In your goodness and wisdom you've given my life purpose and meaning. Not in the way I would've chosen, but in the way you knew best. Thank you, that wherever you place my feet it becomes holy ground. Amen.

THINK ON THESE THINGS

- In your everyday life, what are some of the things you do? What's the difference between what you do and your purpose for doing them?

- Every organization or ministry has a mission statement—its purpose for existence. What is yours? What was God's purpose for each of the following women?
  Moses' sister (Exodus 2:1-10)
  Rahab (Joshua 2)
  Ruth (Ruth 4:13-22)
  Abigail (1 Samuel 25)
  Esther (Esther 4–5)

  If each of these women hadn't done what God had called them to do, how would their choices have affected history?

- Proverbs 19:21 says, "Many are the plans in a man's heart, but it is the LORD's purpose that prevails." What plans of yours are you still holding on to? Pray and ask God to lead you into his higher purpose for you.

- "There is only one relationship that matters, and that is your personal relationship to a personal Redeemer and Lord. Let everything else go, but maintain that at all costs, and God will fulfill his purpose through your life. One individual life may be of priceless value to God's purposes, and yours may be that life."—Oswald Chambers, *My Utmost for His Highest*

EIGHTEEN

When You Get to the Fork in the Road, Take It

GIVE ME DIRECTION

When Grandpa Callaway was sixty-five
he started walking a mile a day.
He's eighty now, and we don't know where he is.

PHIL CALLAWAY

I suffer from a condition known as *directional dyslexia,* but don't bother looking it up in the encyclopedia since I invented it (the term, not the condition). Unfortunately the condition is real. It all started the day I was bothering my dad and he told me to get lost. Ever the obedient child, I did, and I've been getting lost ever since.

I'm kidding about my dad telling me to get lost but not about *getting lost.* I don't know which way is north. I know the sun rises in the east and sets in the west, but I couldn't point it out to you. Orlando and Tampa are both south of me, but I think they're north. I don't know why, but I do. They *feel* northish.

But I'm determined to lick this directional impairment of mine. Last year I took a trip to Tennessee. I rented a car in Nashville with the intention of heading to Clarksville. With my daughter Laura and her friend Chris in the backseat, I pointed my rented blue Neon south...or west...or *somewhere,* following my carefully written instructions to "take I-24 for about an hour until you get to Exit 11." The directions couldn't have been easier or more explicit.

It was *grand.* I drove along, thoroughly delighting in the trip along I-24, drinking in the sights of the trees and the Colonial-style brick houses, enjoying the chatter from Laura and Chris, feeling free and liberated. *I'm driving to Clarksville. I'm a thousand miles from home, and I'm going to Clarksville, la-la-la-la-la.* (Humor me. Unless you've been a forty-three-year-old woman who has never driven farther than a hundred miles away from home, you can only imagine the elation I felt.)

Ah, but too often elation is short-lived. After driving about an hour and a half, it occurred to me that the exit numbers were getting bigger instead of smaller. By the time I passed Exit 84, I even began toying with the idea that I might be going the wrong way. Another clue: I hadn't seen a sign saying "Clarksville" the whole trip.

And it was getting dark.

Not only am I directionally confused, but I'm nighttime befuddled as well. Confused, befuddled, and thrown off-kilter, I forged onward, looking for Exit 11. A voice from the backseat suggested that maybe once the exit numbers reached 100, they started over again at 1. In the dark, a thousand miles from home, I'll believe anything that sounds remotely logical. Unfortunately that theory fell by the wayside around Exit 110. By then I knew that once again I was hopelessly, helplessly lost. So much for la-la-la-la-la.

I had no idea where I was except that I was traveling on I-24 somewhere in Tennessee. I couldn't tell in which direction I was headed or if the road I was on would eventually end up in Kentucky or Georgia. Since I'd never been there before, nothing looked familiar, and the voices in the backseat were too busy talking to each other to be of much help to me in my predicament. Suddenly I was sorry I ever came to Tennessee and berated myself for even thinking I could responsibly drive myself (not to mention my two passengers) to some far-off, distant land like Clarksville. My only consolation was that I had a full tank of gas, and that in the middle of January, it wasn't snowing.

Since I like nothing more than a good metaphor, I've concluded that my entire life is like my excursion in trying to find my way to Clarksville. Even before I left Nashville, I prayed, "Lord, *please* get us there in one piece!" Twenty years earlier I prayed a similar prayer once I discovered I was on my way to heaven. Back then I remember asking the Lord to give me direction and an easy road to travel, hoping that all I needed to do was *go.* That I'd never get lost or end up going around in circles. That my way would be without potholes and forks in the road and I'd never have to travel in the dark. I wanted to know the details of the entire trip in advance so there would be no surprises, plus an estimated time of arrival.

Instead God laughed and said, "Get in the car—you're not even the one driving!" Okay, so this is where my metaphor breaks down, but it's all I have to work with right now, so please humor me some more.

Let's say I'm the one driving the car. (Right here I probably should go into a whole theological explanation of free will within God's sovereignty and how he ordains *everything* in order to bring about his purposes. I could even debate the points of exactly who really drives the car, but I think it'll give us both a headache. Instead, I'll just move on with my story.) For argument's sake, let's say as the driver I know my final destination and have a general idea of the road ahead, but I can't see all its hazards and obstacles. I try using my instincts, but they just get me lost. I follow other drivers who appear to know where they're going, but I hit a Wrong Way sign. I listen to other voices, but they lead me astray. I pass the same Waffle House billboard a million times and worry that I'll never make it. That I'll go over a cliff or crash into a tree.

I'm gripped by panic because I don't know where I'm going or where I am. I turn to the right; I turn to the left. I don't know where to turn! But then I hear a voice behind me saying, "Child, this is the way; walk in it" (Isaiah 30:21, my paraphrase). "This is what the LORD says—" writes Isaiah, "your Redeemer, the Holy One of Israel: *I am the LORD your God, who teaches you what is best for you, who directs you in the way you should go*" (Isaiah 48:17, italics mine).

And so he does.

I remember when I was a new Christian. With fresh faith and a desire to go wherever God directed, everything fell into place. As Barry and I made our final plans to get out of the air force, he found a job with a heating company in Portland, Maine. The company provided him with a van, giving me access to our car. Plus our apartment was only a few miles away from the University of Maine, where I had applied. After fervent prayer, which resulted in wide-open doors before me, I pursued my plans to go to school right away. The only hitch: I had a toddler who needed a baby-sitter. Even that turned out to be only a minor problem because I found a really nice grandma-type lady right away. Everything was set for me to start school. I *knew* it was God's plan. (Why else would everything go so smoothly?)

Now here's the part where, if I were in a car heading to Clarksville, Tennessee, I'd run smack into a *Welcome to Waynesville, Missouri* sign. The government funds I was counting on to pay my tuition didn't arrive as expected. (Colleges frown on students not paying.) I needed that money! Without it I couldn't start school. So I didn't.

I remember being devastated...and perplexed. Bewildered. I had thought I was going the right way—after all, I prayed *and* trusted—but obviously I wasn't going the way God had planned for me to go. His plan was for me to stay home with Alison and be her full-time mom.

Had I gone the wrong way? Had I missed the signs, forced my way through closed doors, violated the Lord's moral principles? No, I had done all the things I knew to be right at the time. Besides, I *had* gone the right way, and I ultimately arrived exactly where God had wanted me to go all along. The twists and turns and dead ends only served a greater purpose.

That's the way life is. If you're in Christ, you're always on the right road, but sometimes it appears that you're going the wrong way. Sometimes you may even deliberately choose to go the wrong way. Or you might meet a fork in the road and have to decide which direction to take, and both are equally good choices. Or you might hit a speed bump and have to slow down, or come to a yield sign that forces you to obey. Sometimes you'll wonder if you've missed the right road completely. Sometimes life's road is so tangled and twisted and filled with obstacles that you'll yearn for the nearest exit. Sometimes you'll just have to return to the place where your trip began.

That's what I had to do in order to find my way to Clarksville. After driving more than two and a half hours, I finally stopped at a convenience store, took my map and my written instructions, and told the clerk, "I'm hopelessly lost!"

He laughed (a common response to which I've become accustomed), then told me, "Lady, you're on the right road, just goin' in the opposite direction." He pointed out that I'd missed an important link of highway when I left Nashville, which put me heading east (or was it west?) instead of whichever direction I was supposed to go. He handed me back my map and said, "Just get back on this road and go straight."

However, by then it was dark, and my jaw hurt from clenching my teeth in frustration. And I was tired and cranky. And my passengers had started voicing serious doubts as to my driving abilities. "You know, God sent fiery serpents to bite the heels of the grumbling Israelites," I reminded them. We needed to go back to Nashville, get something to eat, and start over after a good night's sleep. Clarksville had to wait until morning.

So once again I climbed behind the wheel of my rented Neon, got back on I-24 heading toward Nashville—still missed another two exits—then took a wrong highway. But eventually I made it back to my hotel for the night. The next morning, having made only one wrong turn, we arrived in Clarksville, all in one piece. *Whew!*

So what did I learn from my little Tennessee excursion besides "Always double-check your instructions" and "Don't trust strange voices coming from the backseat"? Hmmm…how about this: If life is a road trip, look straight ahead and keep driving forward. Or as the writer of Proverbs put it: "Let your eyes look straight ahead, fix your gaze directly before you. Make level paths for your feet and take only ways that are firm" (Proverbs 4:25-26). Obey the rules of the road and follow the clearly marked signs. If you feel like you've lost your way, ask for help, but still trust that the detours and obstacles you may encounter are there for a purpose and that the Road Maker designed them especially for you.

Here's some more advice: If you stay alert, eventually you may discover that the road isn't as treacherous in the light as it seems in the dark and that the God who directs you by his Spirit is more than capable of handling any situation that arises. With that in mind, you can relax and enjoy the trip, confident that one day you'll reach your destination, not only in one piece but perfected in the image of Christ.

☙

Lord,

When I don't know where I am, how comforting to know that you do and that because I'm your child, you guide me in paths of righteousness for your name's sake and my best interest. It's you who makes my way perfect. It's you who makes my path straight. Amen.

THINK ON THESE THINGS

- Have you ever been lost? What thoughts went through your head? How did you find your way back?

- When was the last time you "took a wrong turn" in life? What encouragement do the following scriptures offer you?
  Luke 15:11-31
  Psalm 51
  2 Thessalonians 3:5
  Romans 8:1

- Isaiah 48:17 says, "I am the LORD your God, who teaches you what is best for you, who directs you in the way you should go." Write a prayer to the Lord and include these elements:
  Acknowledge his authority and sovereignty as God.
  Give him thanks for his Word, which teaches you what is best.
  Confess your desire to go your own way.
  Surrender to his direction for your life.

- *"...him shall He teach in the way that He shall choose....* If we are saved and sanctified God guides us by our ordinary choices, and if we are going to choose what He does not want, He will check, and we must heed."—Oswald Chambers, *My Utmost for His Highest*

PART FOUR

Show Me

Praise be to the LORD,
for he showed his wonderful love to me.

Nineteen

And in the Center Ring...

SHOW ME MY SIN

Eats anything, but found often feeding on garbage.
Extremely heavy infestations are not uncommon.
MY PEST-CONTROL GUY

I'm trying to get up the nerve to tell you about my sin, but first let me tell you about my cockroaches. It's a fact of Florida life: Everyone has cockroaches in their houses, and to use the technical term, they're *yucky*. They leave trails of brown stuff all inside my cupboards and get inside my file cabinet and mess up my paperwork and make little cockroaches inside my manila envelopes. Even if I try calling them by their more exotic name, *Periplaneta fuliginosa,* or the more common "palmetto bugs," they're still gross.

If I could see them, then maybe I could do something about their disgusting intrusion, but they only come out at night. I don't even know how many we're talking about. Five? Five dozen? Five billion? I have no idea. I don't know if I have a major problem that requires calling an exterminator or a minor one that a few traps could take care of. I simply don't know! I've never seen more than one or two at any one time.

Once I naively thought the one or two I have seen in the daylight meant the problem was limited to only those few, that they were simply bored or lonely and had come out for a little afternoon fun. *Au contraire,* according to the pest control guy who did my last inspection. As he tapped my walls and shined his flashlight into the darkest recesses of my house, he casually remarked that the few I saw were most likely forced out by overcrowding. "Ma'am, for every one you see, there might be two hundred more of them little buggers hidin' and multiplyin' behind your walls," he said as he peered under my kitchen sink.

"But I've only seen a few! Are you sure?" I asked him.

"Trust me, ma'am. They're a whole lot better at hidin' than you are at findin' them."

Still unconvinced, I decided to stay up all night and see exactly how many I really had. Alert and on guard, I waited in my kitchen until I heard the faint rustle of scurrying insect feet. Then in one quick flip, I turned on all the overhead lights. Scores of nasty brown roaches retreated as fast as they could into the tiniest crevices throughout my kitchen.

I had no idea the problem was this bad. As waves of revulsion sent shudders down my back, I knew I had to do something—and fast. So I did what I normally do when confronted with uncomfortable truth that demands action. I hoped like crazy that they would just go away on their own and made a determined effort to forget about it and go on with my life. I crawled back into bed, put a pillow over my head, and vowed never to turn on the lights in the dark ever again.

Now to my sin. First let me say, I'm Not So Bad. In fact, I'm more than Not So Bad. I'm Better Than Many. Not As Good As Some, but not Nearly As Bad As Others. All in all, I'm definitely Not So Bad. That's why I didn't have a problem with the prayer I prayed one Sunday morning in church.

Looking back, I could say it was a moment of temporary insanity. But the more I think about it, it was more like a weak moment of worship (although my pastor says there's no such thing). All I know, I was minding my own business, steeped in mediocrity and completely satisfied with the status quo. *I'm Not So Bad.* Ahhh.

Then we sang, "White as snow, white as snow. Though my sins are as scarlet..." Suddenly I was caught up in the moment, and before I knew it I was praying, "Lord, show me my sin that I might hate it as much as you do." After that I went on to the next song, listened to the sermon, then did what I normally do. I walked out of church and completely forgot about everything.

The following week was a *bad week* (which I'll tell you about later), and that Friday night I was scheduled to speak at a women's dinner at a church out of town. Since it had been such a horrendous week, I relished the chance to get away. Financially, I'd been beyond broke for the longest time, with a stack of almost-due bills on my desk screaming at me to be paid. But this group had promised to "pay me well" as their after-dinner speaker, and the thought of it consumed my entire two-hour ride. *I wonder how much they'll pay me? What exactly does "well" mean? I* have *to sell a lot of books.* Even as I arrived at the church and began meeting people, I kept thinking, *I really need this money.*

Then someone asked me if I'd like some time alone to pray before I spoke. I'm ashamed to admit I hadn't thought about praying. Not wanting to appear unspiritual, I entered a small office and sat on the couch. That's about the time God entered and announced, "I'm here to answer your prayer." An hour before I was scheduled to speak, the Lord Almighty shined his flashlight into my darkness and showed me my sin: that I was consumed to the point of obsession about my overwhelming financial need back home and my hope for escape from it with money earned from this talk. I wasn't thinking about sharing the gospel, only about the money I would receive for sharing it. Not only that, I realized because my need was so great, whatever amount they paid me, it wouldn't be enough, and I knew I wouldn't appreciate it.

Suddenly I wasn't Not So Bad anymore. I wanted nothing more than to scurry into a dark hole like a cockroach, but I had to go out and smile and eat a ham dinner and then stand up on stage to make people laugh and think about Jesus. I faked my way through dinner with polite chitchat. Then I stood to speak. Broken, bleeding, dying from the inside out, *still consumed with getting my check afterward,* I delivered my message. A joke backfired, a story fell flat. Out of the corner of my eye, I spied a bowl of chocolate-covered mints for which I suddenly would have sacrificed my firstborn. And all the while God's spotlight shone on me as I battled my demons and babbled on about forgiveness and restoration, cleansing and hope in Jesus.

When I finished, everyone applauded politely as God aimed his light into another hidden area to reveal Phase Two of my sin. I debated whether or not to tell you about this, but James says, "Confess your sins to each other and pray for each other so that you may be healed" (James 5:16). Because of that, here goes: Normally after I speak, a throng of women gathers around me, heaping praises on me and generally telling me how wonderful, funny, insightful, delightful (blah-blah-blah) I am. Except that night—*no throng*. Only God himself, shining his light, exposing my proud, needy heart, revealing my god of other people's adulation.

I stood there stunned, watching women walk past me as if I were invisible. I felt naked and ashamed, a total failure. All I wanted was to grab my check and go home. After an eternity I packed up my books from the book table (I didn't sell even one), thanked my hostess for a lovely time, and made a beeline for my car, where I could finally find escape and I could comfort myself with having been "paid well." However, to my shock the envelope contained a check made out for only the amount of my expenses. To the penny. That's when it hit me: It was more than I deserved.

It was a l-o-n-g ride home.

Too exhausted to unpack my things when I got home, I fell asleep in my clothes. The next morning as I unloaded my car, still feeling like a failure, I noticed something peeking out from inside my carton of unsold books. A second check, and they had paid me well after all. God had shined his light and exposed my sin, but he didn't leave me without grace. In the middle of my embarrassment and shame he reminded me of his forgiveness, which was there all the time.

So what does this have to do with cockroaches? Nothing. But it has everything to do with a God who cares enough to show me my sin and not let me stay in the darkness. He pinpoints the problem and provides a remedy so my life can be free of filth and destruction. He offers forgiveness for the asking, and cleansing from all unrighteousness. And he blesses me on top of that, especially when I least deserve it.

It's a fact of Florida life: I'm always going to have cockroaches, and I'm always going to have sin. One destroys my house; the other destroys my soul. Both need an expert who knows where to look and what to do about it. How great it is to be free of infestation!

It's good to have the cockroaches taken care of too.

∾

Lord,

If I were to see my sin all at once, it would be too much to bear. Thank you that you only reveal it a little at a time. Even more than that, thank you that you show me my sin because you love me and desire only to make me clean and pure. Amen.

THINK ON THESE THINGS

- In Genesis 3, after Adam and Eve sinned, God walked through the Garden of Eden and found the couple hiding. In what ways do people try to hide their sin? Why do you think they do this?

- When God reveals personal sin, it's never vague ("you're a bad person") but always specific ("you told a lie"). Once sin is revealed, what steps does the Bible say we must take next? (See Psalm 32:5; 1 John 1:9; Luke 19:8.)

- "Show me my sin" is a prayer God *always* answers, although it's rarely pleasant at the time. Read Psalm 51 carefully. What does the psalmist admit about his sin and ask God to do?

- "The bedrock of Christianity is repentance. Strictly speaking, a man cannot repent when he chooses; repentance is a gift of God. The old Puritans used to pray for 'the gift of tears.' If ever you cease to know the virtue of repentance, you are in darkness. Examine yourself and see if you have forgotten how to be sorry."— Oswald Chambers, *My Utmost for His Highest*

TWENTY

Mercy Is a Size-12 Tag on Size-14 Pants

SHOW ME YOUR MERCY

Mercy is deceptive; it is often interpreted as weakness rather than strength.
Yet this weakness has power to change lives.

DAVE LAMBERT

I call them my mercy pants. Casual yet dressy. Roomy, comfortable, hides-a-multitude-of-sins black. Best of all, *I* know they're size fourteen petite, the manufacturer knows it, and God knows it, but if *you* happened upon them hanging in my closet and glanced at the tag, *you'd* think they were only size twelve. I know that's pathetically trivial, but if you're a size-fourteen petite like I am, you take all the mercy you can get.

I call them mercy pants, but I'm not so sure that's what mercy really is. It's not as if I haven't asked for mercy before. I have two brothers who had a fondness for giving Hurts Don't Its. In case you don't have a brother, that's when someone offers what you *think* is a bakery delicacy (a donut), but slugs you in the arm instead while saying, "Hurts, don't it!" After enough of them you learn to beg for mercy automatically at the first sign of a fist.

Aside from the desire to escape my brothers' fists, I never fully understood mercy until an episode of *Little House on the Prairie*. In a nutshell: Son Albert sneaked down to the basement of his sister's school for the blind to take a smoke. His pipe started a fire, which burned down the school and killed his sister's baby. Terrified and wracked with guilt over what he had done, Albert ran away—and Pa ran after him. Albert, thinking Pa would kill him, ran harder and faster, getting more and more desperate with every step. And Pa was right on his heels, like a hunter after his prey.

Finally Albert couldn't go any farther. He heard Pa calling his name, calling him to stop running. Albert couldn't. He was responsible for burning down the school and killing a child. But he couldn't go on. He was trapped! Then Pa called one more time, "Son! I love you!"

I remember watching that with tears streaming down my face, touched to the core of my being, yet unaware that I had just witnessed the mercy of God. All I knew was that I wanted to climb inside Albert's head, and I wondered what it would be like to run from your father like that, *knowing* what you had done (and what you deserved). I wanted to be him, if only to experience the moment Pa shouted, "Son! I love you!" and to feel his father's embrace. But then a cat-food commercial came on and I forgot all about it for a long, long time—until I found myself running and unable to run any longer.

I might as well be up front with you. I've already told you many
of my deepest, darkest secrets. What's one more? I hope we're friends
by now. I already told you I was in the air force, but I didn't tell you
I once stole something: a navy blue, government-issue ("GI"), fur-
trimmed snow parka. Technically you *could* say all I did was "forget"
to return it on my last day of duty, but I didn't forget. I worked in Base
Supply. I had friends who looked the other way while their friends
forged necessary paperwork. Anyway, no one ever checks anything in
the government. (Oops—I hope I didn't just give away a military secret.)
Because of that, it was foolproof.

Except (there's always an "except") a week or two before my enlist-
ment ended I'd given my life to Jesus. Before that the parka-stealing
didn't bother me one iota. But afterward it bothered me big-time.
Unfortunately it didn't bother me enough to return it.

It would've been easy to sneak it back into the clothing-supply
warehouse, but I needed a parka for the coming Maine winter, and I
didn't have one or fifty dollars to buy a new one. So I kept it.

That was in June. I had hoped the nagging Voice inside my head
telling me to return it would go away by July. (It didn't.) The Voice
stayed with me incessantly all through summer and into fall. It was
especially loud during church services and personal prayer time (so I
stopped *that*), and it even followed me into the bathroom. No matter
how I tried to plug my ears, no matter where I tried to hide, all I heard
was a constant, *Return the parka. Return the parka.*

"I'll give it to charity!" I suggested.

You stole it from the air force; you must return it to the air force.

"Can it wait until after the winter?"

Do it now.

"What if I wait until I get a new one? You don't want me to freeze, do you?"

Now.

I still didn't do it. I was too afraid. Afraid of going to jail and wearing stripes (not the most flattering on a size-fourteen petite) and having people know that Nancy Kennedy was a thief.

I felt pursued by the Voice, like an animal in the crosshairs of a hunter's weapon. I couldn't escape it, so finally I gave up and agreed to return the parka and face the consequences, whatever they might be.

The Voice told me to call the head of Base Supply—my former boss—and be honest about what I had done. Although at the time I would've gladly eaten glass instead, I dialed the phone and checked the calendar to estimate how many days of freedom I had left. *Leavenworth, here I come.* Unfortunately this was in the days before answering machines, and I had to speak to my former boss personally.

I took a deep breath and spilled my guts to him. Surprisingly, it didn't kill me. It actually felt good. Then it came time for the axe to drop on my neck. Except (another "except") it never did. Before I made the call I had prayed, "Have mercy on me, O Lord!"

He did. My former boss reminded me that he, too, was a Christian, and he understood sin. But he didn't let me off the hook—I still had to return the parka I stole—but he didn't slap me with a penalty either. He said the matter was closed and would go no further.

I couldn't believe what I was hearing! Surely there must be something I could do to make amends and atone for my sin. "Should I write a letter of apology?" I asked him. "Maybe send you some money—make an anonymous donation to the Pentagon so they could buy a new airplane?"

With firmness in his voice, yet compassion for my plight, he told me simply, "Box it up, address it to me, and be free in Christ. And don't steal anymore."

When I hung up the phone, I was still stunned. I hadn't burned down the blind school like Albert had, but I had received mercy from my Father just the same.

"God's mercy is great," writes author Dave Lambert in *Showing Mercy: Getting What You Give*. "It's greater than the greatest sin. Given freely, no strings attached, it allows us to live without guilt, without self-hatred and without compounding our mistakes." For me, mercy meant no chain gang, no unflattering prison stripes. No groveling or penance to perform. It required restitution but not punishment. Restoration but not public humiliation. *Mercy!*

I understood it for the first time in my life. Deserving the worst but being spared. Not spared to sin again but spared to sin no more. All that was required from me was to accept it as a blessing undeserved. Not to doubt it or to analyze it but simply to enjoy it.

Like a size-twelve tag on a pair of size-fourteen petite pants.

⚬

My Father,

Don't ever let me pray, "Give me what I deserve," for I deserve nothing more than your wrath. How grateful I am that you are a God of mercy and grace and that you extend both to me, an undeserving yet grateful child. Amen.

THINK ON THESE THINGS

- How has God shown his mercy to you in the past? How did you feel? How is he showing mercy to you today?

- Read the following passages from the gospel of John. How did Jesus show mercy in each instance? How did each person respond (or if the passage doesn't say, how do you think they might have responded)?
John 4:1-26
John 5:1-15
John 8:1-11
John 21:15-19 (First see John 18:25-27.)

- Those who have been shown mercy show mercy to others. In your sphere of influence, who do you know who needs mercy? What are some ways you can extend mercy to them?

- "We do pray for mercy, and that same prayer doth teach us all to render the deeds of mercy."—Andrew Murray, quoted in *God's Little Instruction Book on Prayer*

TWENTY-ONE

The Day the Earth Moved

SHOW ME YOUR GOODNESS

I know God is good because he just is.

WESTLEE RHODES, AGE SIX

It's something I'll never forget. Just as game three of the 1989 World Series between the Oakland A's and the San Francisco Giants was about to begin, a quake measuring 7.1 on the Richter scale, with its epicenter forty-five miles from my home, rolled and then shook me, my family, friends, and neighbors for what seemed like an eternity.

At the time, our automatic reflexes took over and the four of us (Barry, Laura, Alison, and I) took cover in the doorway that separated the living room from the hallway. As we rocked and swayed and were treated to a violent roller-coaster ride, not knowing if we would live or die or if the roof would cave in on top of us, as we watched the front door open and close on its own, as our furniture danced and tumbled and the earth roared, all I could say was, "God is so good!"

It was an odd moment of worship, awe, and incredible peace amid chaos, uncertainty, and calamity, with my only thought being: *God is so good! My life and the lives of my husband and children could end at any second—God is so good! We could be homeless and destitute within the hour—God is so good! Lord, you are our future—God is so good!*

After the shaking had subsided and we had taken inventory of each other, my family went to sit down, but I stayed in the doorway. It had become a holy place. A place where God had met me and the ones I love and revealed his goodness. I'll never forget it. It wasn't *after* the earthquake had hit and we were all safe that I was struck by his goodness, but in the middle of the uncertainty. Whatever the outcome, *God is so good!*

Up until that time, I'd asked God to show me his goodness and expected the obvious: the air I breathe, enough food to eat, clothing, shelter, a sunny day for a picnic. He has shown me all that, but even unbelievers give credit to their favorite deity for such blessings. Only Christians give God thanks and proclaim his goodness when it makes no sense to do so. When unbelievers shake their fists at God and shout, "If you're so good, then why did _____ happen?" only Christians can say along with the prophet Habakkuk:

> Though the fig tree does not bud
>> and there are no grapes on the vines,
> though the olive crop fails
>> and the fields produce no food,
> though there are no sheep in the pen
>> and no cattle in the stalls,

yet will I rejoice in the LORD,
    I will be joyful in God my Savior.
             Habakkuk 3:17-18

Since God is not only good to me alone, I've asked some friends to tell me of his goodness in their lives. Here's what they said:

> My husband Dave is dying from Huntington's Disease. This is a rare, devastating, degenerative brain disorder for which, right now, there is no cure. At forty-six years of age, Dave shuffles through his days like an old man of eighty. As his appetite and ability to swallow continue to decrease, so does his weight. Sometimes I am not sure who lives in his body; the three-year-old child, or the old man who sits and stares into space.
>
> Before Huntington's Disease ravaged his brain, Dave earned a Masters of Business Administration degree. Now, the crowning achievement in his life is the day he spent with Goofy at Disney World. With my family of four, I knew I could never afford to take him there. But God is so good. Thanks to the Disney Compassion Program, Dave had his "Goofy Day" at Disney. Although I grieve for the husband I'll never have back, I still know that God is good to me.
>
> —Carmen Leal, author of
> *The Faces of Huntington*

God showed his goodness to me years ago, the night my then-boyfriend came in drunk, tore the house up, put a gun to my head and demanded, "Where is your God now?" At the time I thought I was going to die, but when he passed out, I got in my car and left for good. I lost all my material things that night, but I regained my soul. God is so good!

—Lisa S.

My six-year-old daughter and I lived in a beautiful, spacious, high-rise apartment. We had everything we needed and wanted. My mother took ill the same year my father retired. It was very hard on the both of them in a house alone. So, I built an apartment in their basement and moved in so we could help them both. The cost of building the apartment, plumbing, central air and electrical all took its toll. Yet, in spite of the misfortunes and setbacks, the financial burdens and the lack of privacy, God keeps a song in my heart and a smile on my face. He reminds me that all things work together for good for those who love him. Material things in the world are useless if you are not at peace within your spirit. I don't even have a kitchen, but I never go hungry. Yes, God is truly good!

—Andria T.

It took us a long time to realize it, but God was so good when it came to our first born son. My wife went through a fairly normal pregnancy. When it came time to deliver, though, the normal symptoms weren't there; no labor pains, no breaking water, etc. After four hours in the labor room with no other symptoms except for dilation, the doctor decided that a C-section was needed. Then came the bad news. When they opened Ellen up, they discovered the amniotic fluid was dark green and thick. For three minutes, Shaun didn't breathe. He was rushed to another hospital designed to handle neonatal trauma. So there we were: my wife in the bed, still recovering from surgery, me holding her hand, and both of us wondering what kind of a future our son would have.

We went to Cincinnati seven days later, and through some medical miracle, Shaun was doing great. We got to take him home the next day. But all was not completely well. We noticed Shaun wasn't progressing as a "normal" baby would. At nine months, he was diagnosed with cerebral palsy. CAT scans revealed massive dark blots where normally you'd see convoluted brain tissue. We were devastated. The future looked as dark as those CAT scans.

Today, twenty years later, Shaun is a healthy young man, with an outgoing personality and infectious smile. He relies on a wheelchair to get him around, has very limited vocabulary, needs constant care in feeding, toileting, and cleaning. But through all this, God has been so good. He has given us a son who brings sunshine to those around him and who has a smile and a laugh for just about everyone he sees. That in itself is a small miracle. When Shaun greets friends or even strangers with that smile of his and their faces light up, we know God is indeed so good.

—Harold R.

I was divorced and my son and daughter, ages five and four respectively, were visiting their father. I was sitting with my friend when I suddenly starting pacing back and forth, and told her, "I can't breathe. I feel like something's wrong with Tommy (my son)." Though she was a believer, she looked at me skeptically. "Nancy, nothing's wrong. Calm down!" I waited five minutes, but I knew it was the Holy Spirit warning me. I jumped up and called my ex-husband. He said, "I don't know what's wrong, but Tommy says he can't breathe!" I asked him to bring Tommy right home. While I waited, I got down on my knees and lifted my hands to thank God. I said, "Thank you Lord for being so good!" I took Tommy to the emergency room, where he was given a shot of adrenaline for an asthma attack associated with a cold. The whole time I kept saying, "God is so good. Thank you, Lord." The emergency room doctor thought I was insane.

—Nancy T.

God has been so good in our lives. My husband has kidney cancer, and God has helped us with his pain and the medications necessary to continue on. There are so many others dealing with things far worse than we are, like those who

don't live every day through him and for him. God is so
good!

—Helen J.

My recent bout with dizziness, which I once thought might
be with me the rest of my life, has put me in a place to mar-
vel at God's goodness to me. When I'm dizzy, even the small-
est task requires intense concentration and intense exclusion
of the whizzing world, which is awfully hard with small children in the house. I worried about how I was going to manage the children and the housework. I was facing not being
able to keep my waitressing job, which is paying for school
fees. But even in the midst of doubting whether or not I
could cope, I found that God was good to me. I had no
pain I was capable of doing many things—driving, working at my computer—and I was otherwise well. I still had
all the people and relationships that were important to me.
I slowed down a bit and spent more time on the important
things (like the kids), because some days I could only sit.
Because it was hard for me to sleep, I spent more time with
the Bible. I did things more slowly. I walked slower, talked
more thoughtfully. I got a new appreciation for my health,
my life, and my Lord. And even better than all that, right
when I accepted the fact of being dizzy, I discovered it was
not incurable, and I am well on the way back to steady living!

—"Trickie" from Australia

My husband, Harry, had pulmonary fibrosis and was ill for a very long time. He died on February 29, 1996. God was so good during this time. Since I didn't work outside our home, I was able to spend ten or twelve hours of every day with Harry while he was in the hospital. His doctor even wrote orders so that our little dachshund Kiku could spend every day in Harry's hospital bed with him for the whole week of his last stay, which comforted Harry a great deal. (They were inseparable.) On February 15, Harry came home from the hospital for the last time. Under the care of Hospice, all of the hospital equipment was set up in our family room. His bed faced the television set and we were treated to videos of church services and special greetings from the children in our Christian school.

The evening before his death, as the nurse gave him some water, Harry asked her if it would prolong his life. "No, I don't think so," she said. "Why?"

He answered, "I'm eager to meet my Jesus." He died the following afternoon with his children holding his hands and me tucked in behind him on his bed, hugging him and quietly singing "O Magnify the Lord," which was on the stereo. The very second his spirit left his body the song ended and "There is a Redeemer" began. I felt the gentle hand of God on all of us.

Now I am left with the knowledge that my beloved husband was eager to meet his Lord and that in his last moments he was surrounded by a loving family with Christian music playing as he left us. I can go forward knowing that this was God's plan and that I can be content as a widow and carry on. God is *so* good!

—Jacqui F.

❧

Lord,

I stand amazed at all you have done and continue to do for me. You are good in the earthquake, you are good in the medical emergency, you are good in the death of one of your own. I know that if I never took another unencumbered breath or held a kitten in my hand or kissed my husband or smelled a rose, you would still be so good! Amen.

THINK ON THESE THINGS

- If you were to take a man-on-the-street poll and asked, "How is God good to you?" what are some answers people might give you? In what other ways does God show his goodness to people in general? To other Christians? To you?

- Psalm 119:71 says, "It was good for me to be afflicted so that I might learn your decrees." How has affliction in your life been good for you? What "decrees" did you learn from it?

- Have you ever doubted God's goodness? Meditate on the following scriptures, inserting your name where applicable. Ask God to allow his Word to penetrate your heart.
  Lamentations 3:25
  Psalm 27:13
  Psalm 31:19
  Psalm 34:8
  Psalm 100:5
  Psalm 116:7

- "Often I have heard people say, 'How good God is! We prayed that it would not rain for our church picnic, and look at the lovely weather!' Yes, God is good when he sends good weather. But God was also good [even] when he allowed my sister, Betsie, to starve to death before my eyes in a German concentration camp."—Corrie ten Boom

TWENTY-TWO

A Day Without Sunshine Is Like, You Know, Night

SHOW ME HOW TO LAUGH

The most wasted day of all is that during which we have not laughed.

SEBASTIAN R. N. CHAMFORT

I'd had a bad week. It began the morning I woke up to discover every pair of underwear I own had disappeared. *Every* pair, not just the ones in my dresser drawer. I searched the entire house. Not a trace, not a clue. No underwear. Creepy. *But not a problem,* said I. *I'll just go to Wal-Mart and get some more.*

Except…I didn't have any underwear to wear there. Which meant I had two options: put on a pair of my husband's, or go without. Either way, I knew if I ended up in the emergency room I'd have some 'splaining to do. (I'd tell you which option I chose, but I've already told you more than you probably wanted to know in the first place.)

I'd had a bad week. My neighbor Sandy asked me to feed her dogs and fish while she went out of town. Just stop by twice a day, give them sustenance, let the dogs outside, and then put them in their kennels for the night. *Any idiot can do that*, I thought. So the first day she was gone I went over to her house, fed everyone, and went home.

Later that evening I went back to Sandy's, opened the door to the porch, and discovered I'd forgotten the part about letting the dogs outside. I remembered when I noticed one of the dogs had eaten her couch. Not all of it—he left the springs. Then as I turned around for a millisecond, her other dog ate the entire can of fish food, can and all, and headed for the fish in the tank! When I finally got both dogs corralled and kenneled, I closed the locked front door—with Sandy's key lying safely on her kitchen table and Sandy not due home for another ten days. With visions of dogs' exploding bladders, I roamed the streets of the neighborhood crying, "Marie! Marie!" trying to find the only other person I knew (but didn't know where she lived) who had a key to Sandy's house.

I'd had a *bad* week. I tripped over my cordless phone. When I stepped on the doctor's scale, I found the ten pounds I thought I had lost. I put a carton of ice cream in the pantry. I lost all my marbles.

While explaining my theory that "life could be going down the tubes, but as long as you have great hair everything's peachy," I realized I was talking to a bald man. He failed to find my lame attempt at humor even mildly amusing.

I wrote a racy e-mail letter to my husband and accidentally sent it to about a dozen people in my e-mail directory. While writing a check at the bank, I bit off the end of my pen and ended up with a mouthful of ink. Blue teeth, blue lips, blue gums, blue tongue. Blue drool down the corner of my mouth. Blue fingertips. Blue smear on my white shorts. What made me the bluest was the fact that I had done the same thing once before during a high-school economics final.

I'd had a bad week, although something good did happen. The station manager at our local radio station told me I have a great face for radio! Mostly though, it was a bad week.

My daughter Laura is into the grunge/skater look. She's in the crowd that dresses according to OQ—Obnoxious Quotient. They're the ones with the baggy pants that drag on the ground, the trench coats, and the hair the color of a handful of Skittles. For months we had argued over whether or not she should dye her brown hair blue, compromising instead on bleached stripes, about twelve various shades by the time she got done. It was obnoxious; she was happy.

Then she decided what she really wanted was red hair. *Red—yes! Normal, pretty, ahhh.* I envisioned an auburn dye attaching itself to the blond and gently blending with her brown hair, shining in the sunlight. Breathtaking. So I offered to do it for her.

The good news: The twelve shades of blond stripes were gone.

The bad news: They turned Highway Worker Orange.

The worse news: *She loved it.*

The even worse news: I DID IT.

The EVEN WORSE news: The next day at school, whenever a teacher or someone asked, "What happened to your hair?!" with great pleasure she announced, *"My mom did this!"*

My whole motivation for everything I do in life (basically, to keep people from thinking I'm a bad mom) washed down the shower drain with the dye goop that Laura rinsed out of her hair. But here's the irony: Laura thinks her Day-Glo orange hair is the one and only cool thing I've ever done.

I'd had a bad week and needed a good laugh. I needed a merry heart that does good like medicine (Proverbs 17:22, NKJV). I cried out to God to bring me mirth, merriment, and laughter. A tickle to my funny bone. A pie in someone else's face. Then:

My daughter Alison and son-in-law, Craig, moved to Hawaii for three years.

Barry lost his job.

My car broke down. I had $217 in my checkbook. The bill was $228.

Two magazines I regularly wrote for folded.

I received a letter saying my book *Mom on the Run* is out of print.

Barry and I sat down to figure out our income taxes. For ten glorious minutes, not only *didn't* we owe extra for the first time in seven years, but we were actually getting a refund. *Hallelujah!* But then upon rechecking the math, I discovered a $10,000 error that pushed us into another tax bracket. Our $26 refund morphed before our eyes into a $1,000 debt to the IRS.

That was the final blow. The *coup de grace.* I'd had enough. As life stuck out its tongue and blew me a raspberry, I did the only thing left that I could do: I laughed. Threw back my head and *roared* until tears rolled down my cheeks. For a moment I thought I had lost my sanity, but as I caught my breath, I realized I had actually found it.

"The saint is hilarious when crushed by difficulties," wrote Oswald Chambers in *My Utmost for His Highest,* "because the thing is so ludicrously impossible to anyone but God." Sometimes there's nothing left to do but laugh. Not that laughter changes things—I still owed the IRS $1,000 that I didn't have—but when I laugh about things that are so utterly out of my control, it becomes a surrendering. *I give up, Lord.*

And when my life falls apart around me, when my teeth are blue and my daughter's hair is orange, when my checkbook balance is lower than the sum of my bills, and I line my human frailty up with God's awesome majesty, and I hear his Father-heart chuckling with delight just as I do with my own children, I'm drawn to him. He laughs because he is God. I laugh because I need a Savior. My laughter is my worship. Maybe that's what Reinhold Niebuhr meant when he said, "Humor is a prelude to faith and laughter is the beginning of prayer."[1]

I like the way Phil Callaway, author of *Making Life Rich Without Any Money,* explained his view on laughter in an e-mail message. He told me, "Some things are too good not to laugh about. Me—the biggest sinner I know, the proudest person on earth—going to heaven. *Ha!* Grace reaching me and Jesus loving me enough to die on a cross. *Ha!* While it evokes thanksgiving, it also makes me laugh because it's so implausible." And therefore wonderful.

Phil also mentioned joy being the great note throughout the Bible, and that it's the joy of the Lord that causes us to laugh despite our circumstances. "God has brought me laughter," said octogenarian Sarah when she presented her 100-year-old husband with a baby boy, "and everyone who hears about this will laugh with me" (Genesis 21:6). Some things are so ludicrously impossible to anyone but God that the only response *is* to laugh!

In *Holy Humor,* authors Cal and Rose Samra tell of a person who once approached Baptist preacher Charles Spurgeon with the observation that the gospels don't say that Jesus ever laughed. Spurgeon replied, "To me a smile is no sin and a laugh is no crime. I never knew what the hearty laugh and what the happy face meant till I knew Christ."

I have only one thing to add to that:

Ha ha ha ha ha ha! Hallelujah! Amen.

❧

Lord,

Sometimes life doesn't give us cause to laugh, but you do. Every moment of every day. You created me to laugh, and I can do so because you sit upon the throne. Accept my laughter as my worship to you, my Lord and my King. Amen.

THINK ON THESE THINGS

- When was the last time you laughed? What types of things make you laugh? What can you do to bring more laughter into your life? Do you agree that laughter can be a form of worship? Why or why not?

- Read Psalm 126. What great things has the Lord done for you? Rewrite this psalm as a prayer to God and thank him for all the reasons you have to laugh.

- Proverbs 17:22 says, "A merry heart does good, like medicine" (NKJV). Did you know that one hundred laughs a day is equivalent to ten minutes of rowing or jogging? Go to the library or search the Internet for further research on the health benefits of laughter. How is laughter beneficial physically, socially, psychologically, and emotionally?

- "The world is so full of anguish; life itself sometimes seems so grim. Thank you, God, that in your vast understanding you gave us laughter to make us forget, to restore our wounded spirits, brighten the journey, lighten the load. And surely this too is a clue to your very nature. A nature akin to our own. Thank you for this blessing, Lord. This shining gift of laughter."—Marjorie Holmes, *Who Am I, God?*

---

[1] Quoted in Cal and Rose Samra, *Holy Humor: Inspirational Wit and Cartoons* (New York: Mastermedia, 1996), 32.

TWENTY-THREE

How to Eat an Elephant

SHOW ME YOUR GRACE

Grace comes free of charge to people who do not deserve it,
and I am one of those people.

PHILIP YANCEY

Right now I'm in the process of eating an elephant. Actually, what I'm really doing is trying to learn to dance. (I think eating an elephant would be easier.) The dancing thing is not going well. Basically, I can't do it. It's not that I have two left feet. It's more like my left foot is trying to horn in on what my right foot's supposed to be doing, and I end up prostrate on the floor. Well maybe not prostrate but at least crumpled in a heap. (I'm not what you would call "graceful.")

But I want to be. I want to be *full of grace.* To glide across a dance floor in three-quarter time, in time to the music instead of two beats too late. But when the music bids me go left, I freeze. When I'm supposed to step backward, I don't. And it seems the harder I try, the clumsier I am. Plain and simple: *I can't dance.*

In my struggle to learn, I find I'm at war within myself. Inside I already am a dancer. I'm graceful, free. I turn and stretch with ease as the music flows through every fiber of my being. *I was made to dance.*

But tell that to my feet. When I actually try it, I just can't. Either I'm paralyzed and don't know which way to move, or I'm afraid of who might be watching and who will snicker behind my back (or, horror, to my face).

I remember dancing with my dad as a little girl. How he would pick me up and twirl me around the living room. How I would stand on top of his feet. "Look at me; I'm dancing!" I'd shout to no one in particular. It didn't matter. I was dancing with my daddy.

Then when I got older, we would dance to the rock-and-roll on the record player. I remember one summer night when Dad came in while I was dancing with my brothers, sister, and friend Colleen Gherighty. We laughed hysterically as he kept up with us throughout Iron Butterfly's entire, twenty-seven minute "In-a-Gadda-Da-Vida" and then dove into the pool with his clothes on. You don't easily forget such Kodak moments.

I remember dancing with my friends. We did the jerk and the freddy and made up dances of our own. All through sixth grade I danced with six-foot Gary Davis, my permanent square-dance partner. I watched my mom dance across a stage, tapping to *Washington Square* or rising on her toes as the Sugar Plum Fairy.

I want to dance too! But I'm afraid now. I'm afraid I can't do it. No, I *know* I can't do it. Not like I want to, not like I yearn to. Too much time has gone by. Too much excess baggage. Still, I try, tentatively. In secret. All my past dancing failures haunt me with each attempt. *Remember the time you sat by yourself the entire night because no one asked you to dance? Remember the time you danced with one boy only to discover he wanted to dance with your friend? Remember how that cut you so deeply?*

How could I forget?

Clement Kirk lives in my neighborhood. He's an old guy, eighty-something, but is he spry! *He dances.* I asked him about it once. "What's it like to be on a stage with people watching you? How do you know what to do? What if you mess up?"

He chuckled with delight at my questions. "I just *dance,*" he said.

Then he offered to teach me, but I made up some lame excuse. (I always do.)

"Well, if you ever change your mind, there's a dance studio in town. I could meet you there sometime. You'll love it. I know you will."

He doesn't understand.

I have the desire to dance, but I can't carry it out. What I feel in my spirit and know in my heart is true and right and pure and holy. But my arms and my feet have a will of their own. Still, I give it one more try. I make a few hesitant steps but then falter. That confirms it: Others were meant to dance, but not me.

But the music won't go away. It draws me toward itself. I can't escape it no matter how hard I try. Yet no matter how hard I try to dance, I can't. I just can't.

I did go to the dance studio once. I had to go because the newspaper I write for sent me on an assignment there to write a story about the owner. Normally I'm in control when I go on an interview, but this one was different. I was afraid I would walk through the studio door and find myself naked. That someone would see me and know my shame. That I would be discovered as someone who yearned to be a dancer, who sometimes dared to dream that she could, but who couldn't follow even the most basic steps of the simplest dance.

As I stepped inside the studio, I was greeted (or should I say bombarded?) by my own reflection in the mirrors that lined three of the four walls. It wasn't enough that I had to walk into the studio; now I had to be taunted by images of my own clumsy self. *You don't belong here. You'll never belong here. You're clumsy and awkward and ungraceful. In fact, there isn't enough grace in the entire universe for your feet.*

I battled these and other thoughts as the owner of the studio showed me around, chattering on and on about her students and how much fun they have. I knew all of that already. I'd watched them before. I'd watched *her.* I'd seen her move with grace and beauty, following her partner's lead effortlessly. I wanted to ask her how she does it. I really wanted to ask her how I could do it. But I stayed the ever-objective reporter. At arm's length. Distant. Aloof. Afraid to admit my greatest weakness. Ashamed because I thought she'd know just by looking at me.

She mentioned the word *grace*. It was somewhere in there with the other words: "state competitions," "recitals," "we've been here in town for the last eight years." Maybe she didn't say it. But I heard it.

After the interview I got back into my car, shaking. *Grace.* I knew "For it is by grace you have been saved, through faith—and this not from yourselves, it is the gift of God—not by works, so that no one can boast" (Ephesians 2:8-9). I knew "There is a remnant chosen by grace. And if by grace, then it is no longer by works; if it were, grace would no longer be grace" (Romans 11:5-6). I knew "For sin shall not be your master, because you are not under law, but under grace" (Romans 6:14). I knew all that. But I didn't know how to dance!

I went home to write the story. It was one of those agonizing stories where the words won't come. My notes in my notepad didn't make sense. I couldn't type out a single word, not even the lead, which is normally my favorite part. I just sat at my computer, paralyzed, thinking about dancing, thinking about grace.

I felt unworthy. I've done so much wrong. Sinned too much. Prayed too little. I speak about grace, grace, grace, but I don't live grace. I don't even understand grace. I understand clumsiness and sin. Awkwardness and agony. The need to atone, to do penance. "Therefore, there is now no condemnation for those who are in Christ Jesus," the apostle Paul reminds me (Romans 8:1). But he must be wrong!

Or I must be.

I remember again dancing with my dad. How safe and secure my toddler-heart felt wrapped within his arms. *To my dad, I am a princess,* I think. *He knows the wrong I've done, but to him I'm a princess. I can dance with my dad, trip all over his feet, break his heart, yet my dad loves me. I* know *this to be true.*

I look down at my feet and curse their awkwardness. I type the word grace, then delete it. I don't understand the word. Instead, I think about trying harder. Maybe read a book on dancing. Watch some videos. Go to *Riverdance* or to a ballet. Watch kindergarten children.

I used to dance in kindergarten, I remember. *We had scarves and pretended we were floating in the breeze. Carried along with the wind.* "The wind blows wherever it pleases," Jesus said to a man named Nicodemus, who also wanted to dance. "You hear its sound, but you cannot tell where it comes from or where it is going. So it is with everyone born of the Spirit" (John 3:8). Everyone to whom God calls to the dance.

When you were in kindergarten, I told myself, *you simply listened to the music and let the wind carry you along. What's hindering you now?* I hear the music, and it pulls me out of my chair and away from the story I'm trying to write. Desperately trying to write.

Through my office window I see the oak trees in my backyard sway. It's never windy in Florida! The CD I'm playing, *Pachelbel's Canon in D,* maneuvers its way into my being. *"Dance with me—dance for me,"* I hear the Father whisper to my fearful heart.

"I can't, Lord. I'm too unworthy to dance in front of you."

"My grace is sufficient for you. I know what you've done; I've covered your sin. You stand clean before me, blameless and pure. All I ask is that you dance with me."

I listen to the music of the gospel. "For God did not send his Son into the world to condemn the world, but to save the world through him" (John 3:17). No condemnation for those who are in Christ. *Grace* applied to my greatest failure, my filthiest sin. Grace covering my fixation upon my sin to the neglecting of my Savior, believing his blood to be insufficient. In my focusing on my awkward feet and their imperfection, I've forgotten that all I really want to do is move unencumbered and free. Technique and the perfection of my steps are unimportant. My Father wants me to dance with him. *He wants to dance with me.*

I'm alone in my office. The music beckons. *This is ridiculous,* I tell myself. *Just do it.* So I do. I lift my hands to my Father and take his lead. He holds me close and explains the words to the music I'm hearing. I trip over his feet, I go backward instead of forward, but it's okay. *It's okay.*

I laugh. Oh, how I laugh! It's a moment I've dreamed about my whole life. *I'm dancing.* I'm doing it all wrong, but I'm doing it. I'm dancing with my Father, one step at a time. When the music ends, I'm exhilarated—until I remember the elephant I'm trying to eat.

I turn to my dancing Partner and remind him. This time it's his turn to laugh as he tells me the secret to eating an elephant. *"Child, you eat it the same way you dance. By grace and grace alone, one step, one bite at a time."*

⚜

Lord,

Every breath I take, every heartbeat, every sunset I savor is because of grace alone. Freely given to me, your child, it sets me free to be who you created me to be. Thank you, thank you, thank you for your amazing grace! Amen.

THINK ON THESE THINGS

- Who are some gracious people in your life? What qualities make them gracious?

- Author Philip Yancey asks the question, "What's so amazing about grace?" in his book by the same title. How has God shown his grace in your life? With the help of a concordance, do a study on the word grace, listing all its qualities. (For example, Ephesians 2:8—grace saves us; 2 Corinthians 12:9—God's grace is sufficient.)

- In what area of your life would you like more grace? If you had sufficient grace in this area (which you do if you are in Christ!), what would your life look like? How would your attitudes and actions be different? Repent of your thoughts of "ungrace" and accept God's free gift now. (See Isaiah 30:18 and Hebrews 4:16.)

- "If you have a true faith that Christ is your Saviour, then at once you have a gracious God, for faith leads you in and opens up God's heart and will, that you should see pure grace and over-flowing love. This it is to behold God in faith that you should look upon his fatherly, friendly heart, in which there is no anger nor ungraciousness. He who sees God as angry does not see him rightly but only looks upon a curtain, as if a dark cloud had been drawn across his face."—Martin Luther

TWENTY-FOUR

Glory, Glory, Hallelujah!

SHOW ME YOUR GLORY

But when I see Thee as Thou art, I'll praise Thee as I ought.

JOHN NEWTON

I saw God the other day, only he wasn't where I had expected him to be. I don't know what I had expected, but I know what I *wanted*. I wanted to see his Marvelous Works. I'd been wanting to see them for some time. A big, Holy Extravaganza with Blazing Glory. Evidence of his existence. He'd been silent lately, and I needed to be reminded that he's real. *Really* real. I wanted to see his glory, the same glory that Moses saw. Or that the Bethlehem shepherds saw.

So I started looking for burning bushes and large bodies of water parting and chariots of fire rushing like the wind as they carried ancient prophets to heaven. I looked for miracles or even my daughter cleaning her room without being told.

I looked for God *everywhere*. I found him at the Florida Mall on a bench in front of Barnie's Coffee.

Let me explain something first. On this particular day I *wasn't* looking for God. In fact I was trying to escape him. It was a Sunday. I'd been mean—truly nasty—at home. Snippy, snappy. Nobody did anything to please me. With my bad attitude, I knew I couldn't go to church and take communion. I thought God would surely strike me dead, so I didn't go. Instead of confessing and repenting, I took my daughter and her friend to the mall. Not only did I have a rotten attitude, but I was setting a bad example for my child.

Steeped in my own misery, I parked myself on a bench outside of my favorite gourmet coffee shop and settled down to enjoy a good wallow. Then God came and ruined it all by sitting down next to me and revealing his glory.

He began by reminding me of the early days of our relationship. I'd only been his for a short time when the church I attended in downtown Portland, Maine, invited me to spend a week at their children's summer camp. I'd heard stories of all the fun the adults had, especially the kitchen workers. "You *have* to work in the kitchen!" a woman named Cathy had told me.

Yes! I could envision myself laughing and carrying on and being encouraged in my new faith by seasoned believers. But instead of the kitchen, they put me with Elmer's Glue, the group of staff members' kids who were too young for regular camp, including my own nearly-two-year-old, Alison. They were called Elmer's Glue because everyone had to stay stuck together. Stuck is right. For the next 168 hours, my job was to be glued to ten children under age five—a job I didn't want.

I wanted to be washing spaghetti pots with adults, not wiping noses and backsides of kids I didn't know.

My only ray of hope was the scheduled campfire at the end of the week.

Cathy had told me, "It's the best part of camp—that's when God shows up." She had made it sound glorious, and I wanted so badly to be where God was.

I got through the week only by grace and nap time and by fixing my eyes on Friday night's campfire. *Then* I would see God. But when Friday night came, I couldn't get away from the cabin I shared with the Glue. A little boy cried; my own Alison wouldn't settle down. Someone wet his bunk. And off in the distance I saw the glow of the campfire and heard everyone else's voices. If self-pity were a virtue, I would have been exemplary. *I wanted to be where God was!*

Eventually the Glue went to sleep, but I still couldn't leave. What if one of them woke up...or tried to escape? So I resigned myself to one last solitary evening on the porch stoop.

Then God came.

How do you explain his presence? You can't. He just shows up. You hear the crickets in the woods and watch as an owl swoops through the trees and past the brightest moon you've ever seen. Then a praise song wells up in your soul and you begin to sing, or maybe you recite the words of the Magnificat, "My soul glorifies the Lord and my spirit rejoices in God my Savior." Whatever your response, when God comes, you know that you know that you know you've been visited by your Creator.

Glory!

As I sat on the bench in the mall, God reminded me of yet another time when he showed me his glory. Cathy and I led the middle-school Pioneer Girls group at the same Portland church. Near the end of the year we held a parents' night dinner, with each girl being responsible for bringing a covered dish for the food table. As inexperienced as we were with this age group, we just assumed they would remember. They *didn't*. Some did, but most didn't, and we had a fellowship hall full of girls and parents expecting a meal. I remember Cathy and I hiding in the church kitchen, panicked.

Then God came.

We recalled the gospel account of the five loaves and two fishes which fed five thousand people. Since I was still a novice Christian and not yet jaded in my trust that God would do something for us, I prayed for that same thing to happen to our meager food.

Again, how do you explain how God does what he does? You can't. We finished praying and said *Amen,* then came out of hiding to face our guests. As Cathy invited everyone to help themselves to the food, we saw that everything in the dishes had multiplied. No one else besides the two of us noticed—everyone else was too busy heaping their plates with food that hadn't been there five minutes earlier.

Glory!

Surrounded by shoppers in the mall, I was all alone with God on that bench as he continued to remind me of his glory revealed in my life. Like the time Laura's friend from Tennessee came for a visit. He had two requests: to see the ocean and to go to Disney World. I knew when he asked about Disney World that he didn't realize how expensive tickets are or how broke I was at the time. I told him, "Unless I get a surprise check in the mail or tickets fall from the sky, I don't see how it's possible."

Then God came.

I had told a friend (who also had no money) about my Disney dilemma. It wasn't that I wanted Chris to see Disney; I wanted him to see God's glory. At the time I didn't know how I could show him either one.

That was Saturday. The next day at church, Disney tickets fell from the sky. The friend I'd spoken with the day before approached me after the service with an enormous grin—and Disney passes. She simply said, "These are for you." She had forgotten she even had them, she said, and since her family gets in free through a relative who works there, they no longer need tickets.

Glory once again!

Sometimes God comes and the earth quakes and the waters part, water turns to wine, and boys from Tennessee get to go to Disney World, and all who see stand in awe at the workings of the Lord of glory. But other times God comes and sits on a porch stoop or a mall bench with you as you drink your flavored coffee and feel guilty for skipping communion. He comes at just the right moment, bringing communion with him, and reminds you that you've been his since before eternity. And that he loves you with an everlasting love.

Moses said to God, "Now show me your glory" (Exodus 33:18), and the Lord covered Moses' face as he passed by so the sight of his glory wouldn't kill him. For who could see God and live (Exodus 33:20)? I've never seen the white light of his glory, but I've seen God just the same. When I've cried out for mercy and he's offered it freely, I've seen God's glory. When I've raised my fist to heaven and in a moment of confusion and frustration screamed, "I hate you!" and he's calmed me with his grace, I've seen his glory. When I've not known what to do and he has sent someone to help, I've seen his glory.

I've seen his glory in the faces of my daughters as they struggle to find a faith of their own, and in my husband as he kisses me on the tip of my nose just when I need it most. I've experienced his glory in the laughter shared with friends and in a cup of hot coffee. Glory in the notes of encouragement from my pastor, the hugs and prayers from my friend Linda DeBusk, and in the strings of Bach's *Brandenburg Concerto No. 6.* Glory in the name of Jesus.

Glory in the wise and just answers to my misguided and self-centered prayers—answers I never would have asked for, yet ones I've come to cherish just the same. Like the psalmist, I have seen the Lord in the sanctuary and beheld his power and glory. My heart, too, cries out, "Because your love is better than life, my lips will glorify you. I will praise you as long as I live, and in your name I will lift up my hands" (Psalm 63:3-4).

Just about the time my daughter and her friend finished their shopping, I recalled the words written on a church gymnasium wall in Titusville, Florida. Taken from the Westminster Confession of Faith, it says, "The chief end of man is to glorify God and enjoy him forever." I tucked the thought away and fiddled in my purse for my car keys. The mall was closing. I had seen God.

My daughter left with shopping bags filled with jeans and boxes of shoes, but I left with a heart filled with praise. God came to me and showed me his glory. He reminded me of the life of purpose and meaning he had given me and that I could ask for anything I wanted in his name. So I did. And when I did:

He helped me.

He transformed me.

He gave me all things necessary for life and godliness.

He showed me forgiveness, mercy, grace, goodness, laughter…

…and *glory*.

And I am forever changed.

⸎

Almighty Lord,

You are too marvelous for words! All power, honor, praise, and glory be to you. Someday I will see you in all your glory and splendor, and I will spend forever in your presence. Until then I am content with the glimpses of glory that you send my way. I am so undeserving, and you are Lord. Amen.

THINK ON THESE THINGS

- Psalm 19:1 says, "The heavens declare the glory of God." How is God's glory shown in your surroundings? In your life?

- Read and contemplate 1 Corinthians 10:31. How can you do all things to the glory of God? Make a list and offer it up to the Lord as an act of worship.

- Rewrite Psalm 111, 113, 138, or 146 as a personal prayer of praise to the Lord.

- "Here is the secret to a life of prayer. Take time in the inner chamber to bow down and worship; and wait on Him until He unveils Himself, and takes possession of you, and goes out with you to show you how a man can live and walk in abiding fellowship with an unseen God."—Andrew Murray, quoted in *Pathway to the Heart of God*

About the Author

What could I possibly say about myself that I haven't already? I grew up in Southern California and joined the air force when I was nineteen, *just to find a husband*. It worked! My husband's name is Barry, and he's cute as a button. We have two daughters (Alison and Laura) and a son-in-law (Craig). I adore them all. Currently I live in central Florida where it's hot. My goal is to see how long I can go without wearing a bathing suit.

In case you want to know what I do besides drive girls around, for the past seven or so years I've written a weekly (sometimes weakly) feature article for the *Citrus County Chronicle* religion page. For the past two years my articles have won First Place in Religion Feature Writing from the Florida Press Club, which is kind of cool. Mostly I like hearing about and writing stories of how God is changing people's lives. I've also written other things. Maybe you've seen my articles in magazines such as *Marriage Partnership, Christian Reader, Virtue, Aspire, Christian Parenting Today,* and a bunch of others. A few years ago I wrote three books *(Help! I'm Being Intimidated by the Proverbs 31 Woman, Mom on the Run*, and *Honey, They're Playing Our Song)*, but now they're out of print. Too bad, too. You might have liked them. Oh, I've also done some speaking in the past few years at dinners and retreats. I don't know how good I am, but I always have fun.

Here's where I should put all my degrees and titles, but I don't have any. Instead, I'll use this space to thank you for buying my book—I desperately need a new car. If you'd like to contact me (not about a new car, unless you happen to have an extra one sitting around), you can reach me at: Nancy Kennedy, c/o Seven Rivers Presbyterian Church, 4221 W. Gulf-to-Lake Hwy., Lecanto, FL 34461.

A TEST OF WILL

A TEST

WARREN MACDONALD

With contributions by Geert van Keulen.